WOMEN ATHLETES TALK ABOUT
SPORTS AND THEIR FAITH

Competitor's Edge

Dave Branon

MOODY PRESS
CHICAGO

PHOTO CREDITS:

Michelle Akers	Courtesy: Reebok
Rhonda Blades	Chuck Solomon/Courtesy: WNBA Photos
Ruthie Bolton-Holifield	Courtesy: WNBA
Amanda Borden	Courtesy: David Moss/Images Professional Photography©
Kim Braatz-Voisard	Courtesy: Silver Bullets
Jean Driscoll	Courtesy: Jean Driscoll
Mary Joe Fernandez	Courtesy: Corel WTA Tour
Jackie Gallagher-Smith	Courtesy: Jackie Gallagher-Smith
Kathy Guadagnino	Courtesy: LPGA
Nancy Lieberman-Cline	Courtesy: Nancy Lieberman-Cline
Lavonna Martin-Floreal	Courtesy: Lavonna Martin-Floreal
Barb Mucha	Courtesy: LPGA
Charlotte Smith	Arie Crabb/Courtesy: San Jose Lasers
Rosalynn Sumners	Courtesy: IMG
Sheila Taormina	Courtesy: Sheila Taormina
Wendy Ward	Courtesy: LPGA

ISBN: 0-8024-7819-0

1 3 5 7 9 10 8 6 4 2

Printed in the United States of America

To the 1997 Grand Rapids Baptist High School girls basketball team, who personify the good sportsmanship, hard work, and Christian testimony that is represented in the women in this book.

To the women athletes in my life: Lisa, who never stopped running in high school; Julie, who shares my love for hoops; and Melissa, who surprises us with her basketball prowess. And Sue, who is a world-class co-coach of our team. My son Steven and I appreciate the women in our life.

Competitor's Edge

Contents

Acknowledgments

A lot of people think interviewing athletes is all fun and games. Sometimes it's about as much fun as coaxing an oral book report out of a reluctant seventh grader.

That's not the case, though, with the women I talked with for this book. Refreshingly candid and outgoing, these top women athletes made the process easier than I expected. Having mostly interviewed men for my previous books and articles, I found the change invigorating. Sure, there are talkative male sports figures like Rex Hudler. And there are guys who are eager to speak boldly about their faith, like A. C. Green, but it was nice that across the board the women I talked with for this book were friendly, open, and cooperative. So, my first thanks goes to them for their eagerness. By the way, all of the women in the book provided interviews without any remuneration.

And then there are the people who helped me get in touch with these ladies.

A hearty thanks goes out to the following:

For *Michelle Akers*, thanks to my friend Judy Nelson for hooking us up.

For *Rhonda Blades*, thanks to Victor Lee, who prompted Rhonda to get in touch with me.

For *Ruthie Bolton-Holifield*, thanks to Andrea Lepore of the Sacramento Monarchs for making connections.

For *Amanda Borden*, thanks to Lynn Ruhl at the Cincinnati Gymnastics Academy for her assistance. Also, thanks to Patty Borden for her cooperation in helping me talk with Amanda.

For *Kim Braatz-Voisard*, thanks to Ashley at the Colorado Silver Bullets for finding Kim for me.

For *Jean Driscoll*, thanks to my friend Jennie Chandler for letting Jean know I needed to talk with her.

For *Mary Joe Fernandez*, thanks to Veronique Marshal of Corel WTA for lining up the interview.

For Jackie Gallagher-Smith, thanks to Eddie, her husband, for getting us together.

For Kathy Guadagnino, thanks for being available for me to call.

For Nancy Lieberman-Cline, thanks to her friend Rhonda Blades for the good recommendation. And thanks to Angie in Nancy's office for her help.

For Lavonna Martin-Floreal, thanks to Roxanne Robbins for letting me talk to your good friend.

For Barb Mucha, thanks for letting me call you directly.

For Charlotte Smith, thanks to Shana Daum in the San Jose Lasers' office for her help.

For Rosalynn Sumners, thanks to Julie in Jay Odgen's office for being so efficient and accommodating.

For Sheila Taormina, thanks to Chris Godfrey for putting in a good word for me.

For Wendy Ward, thanks to her agent, Steve Loy, who made sure I got in touch with her.

And, as always, thanks to Rob Bentz at *Sports Spectrum* for his interest and advice. The *Sports Spectrum* archives and files are always a major source for a book like this.

Introduction

Do you consider the advent of women's sports to be a relatively new phenomenon? Do you think the idea of girls and young women dribbling a basketball or slugging a softball is a twenty-first century kind of thing? Many people do.

But that's not the way it has been in my family.

Girls in my family have participated in sports since before World War II. We've accomplished what is, I think, a relatively unusual three-generation record.

I discovered this recently when my mother was showing me her high school yearbook. As I leafed through the pictures of students from an era I had not known, I saw something I never expected.

My mother was a basketball player. I was a bit surprised to know that high school girls' basketball even existed in 1939. Yet there was the team picture, and there was Mom. A bit younger than I had ever seen her—but it was her all right.

Now jump ahead one generation to my sister, Alice. She kept the hoops string going when she played college basketball at Tennessee Temple University in Chattanooga. Her game was a bit different from the one young women play today; she played six-person basketball.

That brings us to a new generation. First my mother. Then my sister. And now my daughter, Julie, whose love for basketball and dedication to it has driven her to play the game year-round for several years—very much like I did as a kid. All told, I've watched her play in well over 100 games from seventh grade through varsity. And that doesn't count the numerous Amateur Athletic Union and three-on-three tournaments in which she participated.

For her, it has become second nature. Nobody thinks twice when she tells them she's a basketball player.

The fact that women are playing sports is not new. But something is fresh and exciting and vibrant about today's female athletics. Today their efforts are receiving wider acceptance, being watched by more people, being supported by more money, and producing thousands more participants.

The simple fact that one high school girl in three is an athlete is a clear indication that a new era has dawned in women's sports.

For further verification, look at what happened in 1996—perhaps the watershed year in women's sports.

- The US Olympic basketball team swept past all obstacles to become the greatest women's team in the world—maybe the greatest ever.
- The US Olympic women's soccer team solidified their claim on the top spot in the world game by winning gold in Atlanta.
- The US Olympic softball squad made it a trio of women's dominance when they stood atop the gold medal platform.
- The American Basketball League made the best effort ever to present a strong, well-financed pro basketball league for women. At the same time, the NBA put its remarkable marketing skills behind the WNBA, which began play the following summer.
- The LPGA continued to increase its purse for the women's game.
- Seven young women from the US captured the world's heart when they surprised everyone at Atlanta by winning the gymnastics gold medal.
- Women's college basketball continued to defy the naysayers by attracting larger crowds—both in the arenas and on television.
- Tennis brought along new stars of the future such as Martina Hingis and Venus Williams—women who gave a lift to a game some had begun to think was slipping in popularity.

What does this all mean? First, it means that the opportunities for women to use sports as a career catalyst are growing to levels that may someday rival the opportunities for men. With the increasing popularity of women's sports come new job possibilities: coach, trainer, broadcaster, front office administrator, sportswriter, athlete, athletic director, public relations person, advertisement writer, and on it goes. The growth of women's sports has a ripple effect through the economy as women seek new roles in sports.

Second, and more important, Christian women are now getting to enjoy the benefits of using sports as a tool for telling others about Jesus Christ. What was once a mostly male domain now offers avenues for women. There have always been some outlets, such as Athletes in Action, which sponsors evangelistic teams in both men's and women's basketball. But now new opportunities are arising.

For instance, Michelle Akers, who was one of the leading women on the US soccer team that took the gold in 1996, has written two books that allow her to give her testimony. Rhonda Blades, who hit the first three-pointer in WNBA history, uses her story to attract attention so she can talk about her faith. And Jane Albright-Dieterle uses the respect she's gained as the wildly successful basketball coach at the University of Wisconsin to earn a hearing about her relationship with Jesus Christ.

The women in this book have tasted enough fame to realize that they can touch hearts by telling their stories. They know that God has blessed them with their ability at just the right time—at a time when more and more sports fans are turning to women's sports. And at a time when their remarkable success makes their stories ones we want to hear.

These women and thousands of others are pioneers, in a sense. They are pounding against the traditional thinking that women athletes are not skilled, strong, or knowledgeable enough to stand on their own. They still fight that old Bobby Riggs–Billie Jean King syndrome that says if they can't beat the guys one-on-one, their game isn't worth watching (and, by the way, many of them can do that). But that tired dictum usually falls harmlessly to the ground like a discarded hairclip these days.

From someone who has watched hundreds of girls' and women's basketball games and who has marveled at the athleticism of women like Mary Lou Retton, Cheryl Miller, Flo-Jo, Gail Devers, Betsy King, Steffi Graf, Cynthia Cooper, Jean Driscoll,

Picabo Street, Kristi Yamaguchi, and hundreds of others like them, believe me, women's athletics is incredible. It must offer no apologies. It is legitimate to the max.

That's why I'm proud and excited to bring you the stories of many of today's top women sports figures in a variety of sports. Their candor is refreshing, their eagerness to talk about their faith is encouraging, and their stories are all challenging.

No, women's sports is not new. Yet it is moving into a new, stronger era. Keep an eye on these women—and watch for new ones coming along to replace them. You'll agree that these competitors have an edge—an edge that comes from a heart that is set on achieving excellence for God. Enjoy their stories.

Michelle Akers
1996 Olympic Gold Medalist: Soccer
HEART OF A CHAMPION

VITAL STATISTICS

Born: February 1, 1966, in Santa Clara, California
Height: 5'10"
College: Central Florida University
Single
Residence: Orlando, Florida
Special Interests: Hiking, climbing with her dad; promoting education about Chronic Fatigue Syndrome; sports ministry

CAREER HONORS

1981–84: Three-time high school All-American
1985–88: Four-time college All-American
1985: Member of first-ever US Women's National team
1985: ESPN Athlete of the Year
1988: Hermann Trophy (best college soccer player)
1990, 1991: USOC Female Player of the Year
1991: Member World Cup champion US team
1991: Golden Boot winner at World Cup; leading scorer
1992: Swedish pro league Tyreso FF Elite, Top scorer
1996: Member Olympic gold medal US team

OTHER HIGHLIGHTS

More than 100 caps (international competition)
All-time leading scorer in international competition for US teams
(men and women)
No. 10 jersey retired by Central Florida on February 1, 1992

WARMING UP

Michelle Akers would be the first to admit that she did not make it through the Olympic Games in 1996 on her own. "I had a whole nation praying for me," she says. "That's the only way I made it through the tournament. I had my grandmother and her church praying for me back in Washington. I had all the people of my church in Orlando praying for me. I had people in Campus Crusade for Christ. I knew something other than myself was making it happen. I knew I wasn't carrying myself. The people's prayers were holding me up."

FAVORITE BIBLE PASSAGE

This is the word of the Lord to Zerubbabel: "Not by might nor by power, but by my Spirit," says the Lord Almighty (Zechariah 4:6).

Michelle Akers

Ever have one of those days when you just don't want to swing your feet over and land them on the bedroom floor? When just opening your eyes seems like a day's work? When you feel like you couldn't run water, let alone run up and down a soccer field?

Michelle Akers has those kinds of days all the time.

Days when, as she describes it, "you feel like a battleship, like you weigh five million pounds."

That might be an easy problem to deal with if Michelle had a job where she sat at a desk all day editing a newspaper or auditing somebody's finances. She might not have such a struggle if her most strenuous activity were speed-walking to the lunchroom or power-lifting the telephone receiver.

But what Michelle Akers does with that virtual battleship she carries around is nothing short of amazing.

She whips her body around a soccer field playing with the best players in the United States as they defend their goal against the best teams in the world. The most unusual thing of them all is that when all things are considered, Akers herself is one of the best soccer players on the planet.

And one of the gutsiest.

Michelle Akers has Chronic Fatigue & Immune Dysfunction Syndrome (CFIDS). And a gold medal from the 1996 Olympics.

Go figure.

Everyone gets tired after playing a tough game of soccer. Michelle's problem is that she is tired *before* she plays. For long periods of time. Without a remedy.

No one who has watched Michelle play soccer would describe her as "tired." From the time she switched from football (her goal in life was to play for the Steelers until a teacher told her that girls don't play football) to soccer, till the time she stood on the podium to receive her gold medal in 1996, Akers has played the game with the abandon of a unbroken colt.

Before she developed CFIDS, at times she had coaches who had to tone down her aggressiveness, lest she get hurt. And it was not just in games that she was gung-ho. Even in her training, she was noted for working out far longer than any other person on her team.

Michelle came by her hard work and determination naturally. As she was growing up in the Seattle area, she observed that her mom and dad were pillars of strength. Her dad, Bob, who worked as a meat cutter by day and earned a degree in psychology by night, didn't let his agenda interfere with his interest in Michelle or her brother, Mike.

"My dad and brother and I spent many hours in the backyard playing soccer or football. Or we were skiing or hiking," Michelle says. She recalls the hours and hours he spent on the sidelines watching her games—no matter how much Seattle rain was falling.

Although Bob Akers supported his daughter's soccer pursuits, he was afraid that it might not bring the results that her relentless efforts deserved. "My dad's biggest fear was that I would get to the point where I would outplay the game and that I would be disappointed by something I had given my life to."

Of course, how could he know that such things as world championships and Olympic medals would eventually become a possibility for Michelle? In the early '80s, neither of those opportunities seemed reasonable for any American girl.

The influence of Michelle's mom on her soccer life was also extremely significant. "Initially, it was my mother who got me into soccer." Even before it was fashionable, Ann Akers was a middle-class soccer mom.

She was also something else before it was fashionable. She was the first female firefighter in Seattle. "She did a lot of things that normal women didn't do," Michelle says of her mom. "So I kind of had this mentality that I could do anything I wanted. It never crossed my mind to think, *Well, I'm a girl, I can't do that.* To have a mom who lived that way helped."

That may have helped Michelle in her early days of soccer when she often played on boys' teams. "Usually, I was the only girl playing with a bunch of guys. I preferred playing against the guys. Some of the parents were asking, 'What's she doing out there?' But when they saw that I could play, I was accepted right away."

With her parents behind her, Michelle dived headlong into soccer—not for the glory, not for the awards, not for the recognition it would bring her. She simply played because she loved the game. "I just said, 'I'm playing.' I loved it."

And Shorecrest High School was glad she did. During Michelle's four years on the varsity there, her team won one state championship and several Metro Conference titles. For her part, Michelle was named All-American three years in a row. "As I proceeded through my career, all of a sudden there were college scholarships available."

The kid who played soccer for the love of it was starting to reap the benefits of her skill.

After high school, Michelle took her boundless energy to Central Florida University, where she impressed her teammates with her self-control and determination. When she arrived, she was something of a legend—and many of her new teammates were a bit in awe of her. Yet her lack of ego won them over. In fact, she confided in one teammate that she was not sure she would even make the team.

Also impressive was her method of dealing with disappointment. After a loss (which was rare at Central Florida) or some bad news, Michelle didn't rearrange the locker room in a fit of rage or redistribute the contents of her gym bag in anger. She ran. One time, after hearing that the team had not received a seemingly deserved berth in the NCAA tournament, she ran nine miles while her teammates were back at school ranting and raving.

Miss Energy rambled through her soccer career, continuing to pick up honors and selections to elite teams. While at Central Florida, Michelle was named the winner of the initial Hermann Trophy for women, which is now given annually to the best college player in America. Heisman, Hermann. Different sport. Same idea.

Another first for Akers was her selection as a member of the US Women's National team—the first such team of Americans ever put together.

In international competition for the next several years, Michelle continued to shine. In fact, between her college days and the 1991 FIFA Women's World Championships, Michelle scored forty-two goals in forty matches. At the FIFA fete that year, though, Akers showed the world why she was perhaps the best soccer player anywhere.

In the tournament, Michelle scored ten goals to lead the Americans to the World Cup title. In one game, against Taiwan, she scored five times. And in the final game, against Norway, Michelle single-handedly outscored the Norwegians two-to-nil.

The World Cup victory and Michelle's incredible success suddenly lifted her into a new and unfamiliar position. For much of her life since she had been named an All-American soccer player as a sophomore in high school, the soccer world knew who she was. But winning the World Cup turned her into a major star both in soccer and in the new world of endorsements.

Michelle signed a deal with Umbro and was soon jet-setting around the country making appearances. Meanwhile, she continued to play soccer and dominate games on the national and international level. Nothing, it seems, could stop her.

Nothing did until she collapsed in 1993 while playing in San Antonio, Texas. Soon she was diagnosed with CFIDS, and her life changed. The woman who trained so relentlessly and played so aggressively now faced a battle just to compete.

Many people would have quit. After all, with what she had accomplished, Michelle could easily make a living as a coach or as a soccer expert.

But there were still some goals on the horizon. There was the World Cup to defend. And there was another new opportunity. Soccer would be a medal sport for the first time at the 1996 Olympics. For Akers, it was no time to quit.

It was, though, time for some changes.

Despite the incredible success Michelle had achieved in soccer, her life was anything but world-class. Besides the debilitating effects of her Chronic Fatigue, Michelle was suffering the results of spiritual illness as well. In fact, she was in critical condition spiritually.

When she was a high school student, a teacher named Al Kovach had led her to faith in Jesus Christ. "I could clearly see Christ in him," Michelle recalls. "That was the first inkling I had that Christ was different from other notions I had about being a Christian. Mr. Kovach was altogether different. What he had, I wanted."

What Michelle had seen of Christianity before was "totally weird," as she says. Although she had attended church with her godly grandmother and grandfather (Grandma played the organ; Grandpa was an elder), she was not convinced that being a Christian was what she wanted. "My idea of a Christian was someone who was stiff and boring. Never smiled. Very rigid. Lots of rules.

"I thought, *How can I have fun? I don't want to be involved in something like this.* If I had a soccer game on Sunday, I was psyched because I didn't have to go to church."

Then along came Mr. Kovach, and things changed. For a while at least.

When things kept going her way because of soccer, Michelle walked away from her relationship with Christ—leaving Him behind to pursue her own agenda.

"As a kid in 1982, I was looking for Christ to be a helicopter pulling me out of a situation. And He did. But I didn't understand where to go from there. I think that's why I went back to my own way. It took everything to crumble and fall apart, for me to be broken, before I knew what I should do."

In 1994, Michelle Akers—world champion soccer player, bigtime soccer spokesperson, and all-around great person—was in trouble.

Her career was in question because of CFIDS. Her spiritual life was nonexistent. And her four-year marriage was in shambles. "I was empty and almost hopeless."

That's when she began to get some help from some friends.

"Some key people helped me at that point. One of my best

friends was Steve Slain, a massage therapist and strength coach. He was with our team during that last year when I was falling apart.

"We were at the end of our tour with the national team. My husband and I had decided to divorce, and I was going to go away into the mountains for two weeks to be by myself." The Akers family has a cabin in the Cascade Mountains, and Michelle knew it was a perfect place of refuge—a place to try to put life back together.

When Sloan heard that Michelle was going to the cabin, he said to her, "Before you go, why don't you go to church with me?" She says, "At church I heard about relationships—how your relationship with Christ reflects your relationships with others. How you need Christ to develop strong relationships with others. I was convinced that was the answer. I decided that this was what I needed to pursue first before the other stuff could get squared away.

"Also, Steve gave me some sermon tapes to listen to while I was up there at my dad's cabin in the mountains."

While at the cabin, Michelle realized that "Jesus is a person, and you have to have a relationship with Him—one that you can experience on a personal level."

Also while on her sabbatical, Michelle visited her grandparents' church, where she heard a sermon about a family who had been called into missions. The pastor mentioned the importance of serving God with the special talents God has given. As she listened, Michelle knew the message was aimed at her.

She realized that God was calling her to use her fame as a soccer star as a way to witness for Him.

From then on, this would be Michelle's goal—to let people know that she played in God's power and for His glory.

This turnaround in her spiritual life, however, did not result in a corresponding turnaround in her physical condition. She still had to battle Chronic Fatigue every day in order to compete.

The next two major events on Michelle's soccer calendar were the two biggest events in the world of that sport. First, in 1995, she and her US teammates went to Sweden to defend their 1991 World Cup title. Relentlessly, Michelle trained and battled her illness—knowing that this time the US team would be a target. Everyone wanted to defeat the defending champion.

As the time neared for the event, Michelle backed her training program down a bit to conserve her energy. And she turned the events of the tournament over to God, asking for His strength.

Unfortunately, the 1995 World Cup did not turn out as well for the US as the 1991 tourney had. For starters, Michelle received a serious injury just six minutes into the first game against the Chinese. As Michelle went up to head a ball, a Chinese player banged heads with her, sending Akers crashing to the stadium turf. As she fell unconscious, Michelle twisted her knee. She did not play full strength the entire tournament, and the US lost in the semifinals to Norway.

With that disappointment behind them, the US team now could focus on the summer of 1996 and the second event—the Olympics. And Michelle had to crank things up one more time as she sought gold.

"I went into the Olympics thinking, *I've been through this stuff before. It's not going to be much different from the other world championships I had played in.* But that thought was completely blown away. It was so different."

Michelle had experienced a variety of other people's responses to past soccer success by the US team, but for the most part, the response had been apathy. Even after winning the World Cup in 1991, Michelle and her teammates came home to a country that was mostly oblivious to their accomplishment.

But in 1996, Michelle discovered that the addition of the word Olympics to an event made it truly special.

"I didn't realize the magnitude or the depth of passion the American public had for the Olympic Games," she says. "We had missed that before in the two World Cups because we were playing overseas, and the World Cup is solely soccer. But at the Olympics, there was an incredible amount of people who were involved in the Games, and the awareness people had for the Games was great.

"The soccer fans were just nuts. People who weren't soccer fans were there. The World Cup wasn't promoted, so no one knew what was going on unless you were hard-core soccer fans. But not with the Olympics. The emotion and awareness of the Olympics kind of overwhelmed me."

For Michelle, who now calls Orlando home, there was a special bonus in 1996. Two of the games were played in her hometown. "We played two games in Orlando, one in Miami, and two in Athens.

"In Orlando, I remember standing in the tunnel waiting to go out. First, it's the kickoff game for my first Olympics. Then, I'm playing in my hometown. I have a lot of people who had put a lot of effort into keeping my body in one piece so I could play in these games. Walking out to that, to be able to play, it was quite a feeling. It was quite a feeling to know you are in your hometown and people are cheering directly for you."

Michelle's illness meant that she could not enjoy the entire atmosphere of the Games. In fact, she felt a bit isolated during this time. "The only thing I could do was play, then drop dead afterward," she says.

"I was so focused on hour-by-hour, minute-by-minute keeping track of what I had to do to compete. I couldn't afford to take my eyes off that. Because I was so isolated, it wasn't until I looked back that I understand how great the Olympic Games were.

"I was on a very regimented diet. I could only eat certain things. We had to arrange with the venue concerning the foods I had. My meals had to be cooked differently from the others on my team. After the matches, they had IVs ready for me. I would be taken off the field and into the training room to get IVs for two hours while everyone else was visiting with their families at the postgame reception. The next day, the only thing I could do was eat, rest, and get my body working again.

"Then, when you're on the field, you feel weighted down. You're foggy brained. You just want to stop. You are fighting your body just to keep going."

It's enough to make most people give it up. Why subject yourself to such a regimen? Why not just give in to Chronic Fatigue, and call it a career?

Because Michelle Akers loves the battle. "I'm sick in that way," she says. "The bigger the challenge the more fun I have. I would go into the match not feeling good, and I would try to adjust how I was feeling to the kind of player I would be that day. I knew full well that I was going to be very sick afterward and not be able to function the next day. Still, I would go out and try to play as long and as well as I could. That is a weird feeling. During the game, you're pushing and pushing and you're trying to gather every ounce of energy that you have. In a way, it's hard. I've got all these odds against me. Will I quit or will I drop?"

Michelle wouldn't quit. She had too many people depending on her. She had too many people who had worked hard to make her strong enough to play. And she had all those people praying for her. "I knew I wasn't carrying myself. The people's prayers were holding me up."

It was old-home week for Michelle as she and her teammates checked in to their facilities on the campus of Central Florida University, where they stayed during the Olympics.

Akers showed her dedication to the team by missing out on one of the most thrilling parts of the Olympic experience—Opening Ceremonies. Afraid to expend the energy, she stayed back at the village.

The first game for the US was a bit of a breeze as they swept past Denmark 3-0. Michelle was replaced with twenty-eight minutes to go in the game, leaving to a standing ovation from the hometown crowd at the Citrus Bowl. From the time the game ended until the next game with Sweden two days later, Michelle's time was taken with trying to get her body ready to play again.

There were IVs and ice packs and a special diet and a rigid schedule of rest. While others were able to enjoy free time on the town, Michelle stayed in the training room, trying to muster enough strength for another ninety-minute showdown.

For the next two games, Michelle played each of those ninety minutes. Carrying around that body that felt like a battleship, she refused to go down.

In game two, the US beat Sweden 2-1, and in game three in Miami, the Americans tied China 0-0.

Next, it was on to Athens, Georgia, for the final round of games for the Olympians.

Again Michelle had done nothing but rest, get IVs, and try to store up enough energy for the next game. As the semifinal match against Norway neared, Michelle feared that she couldn't make it. Her fatigue symptoms were more severe each game, and her recovery was less effective. Although she had no thoughts of not going on, she was not sure how far she could go.

At half-time, the US team was down one goal to Norway, 1-0, and Michelle was down to empty in her energy tank. Steve Sloan worked over her slumped, depleted body—encouraging her to keep going and trying to get something into her stomach that would give her some energy. All Michelle could do in the locker room was pray.

Back and forth the teams went in the second half, protecting their goals flawlessly. With just ten minutes to go, the US was awarded a penalty kick. At this point, Michelle was so gone physically that it took her a few seconds even to figure out what was happening. Realizing that the US had a scoring opportunity, she indicated that she wanted the kick.

Newly revived by the opportunity, she booted a goal past the Norwegian goalkeeper to tie the score at 1-1. That score stood as the final whistle blew.

The game headed into overtime. Sudden death.

Michelle, who looked and felt like death, told her trainer that she couldn't play anymore. He ignored her, stuffed more Power-Ball bars and Gatorade down her throat, and sent her back onto the field.

Minutes later the US scored, and Michelle Akers had played her third straight complete game.

Then came the finals. Going for the gold.

The US versus China.

As Michelle thinks now about that game, she says, "The gold medal game was a complete haze. That was not a fun game for me. We played China, who is extremely fit, very talented, very skillful. They hold the ball a lot. So when you play China, you basically run and run and run. At twenty minutes into the game, I was ready to come off. I didn't think I was going to be able to make it. At half-time, I thought I was done for sure. I thought, *I'll just keep going until I drop*, and I never dropped." Again, Steve Sloan, PowerBalls, and prayer kept her upright and kicking.

In the second half of the tied gold-medal game, American Tiffeny Milbrett poked a goal past the Chinese keeper for the winning point. The US won 2-1, and the celebration began.

"Afterward, the highlight was standing at the podium," Michelle says. "When I was on the podium, I was so quiet inside.

So quiet. Grateful. Humbled. I recall looking back at the minute-by-minute choices I had to make when I was on the field and then off the field when I wasn't feeling well to keep going no matter what. Standing there, I was able to trust God enough to know He had me there for a reason. His power had enabled me to get this thing done."

"The Olympics was an incredible moment. It helped me realize that I could trust God for everything. Before I turned my life over to Him, soccer had been the most dear to me of everything. It was who I was. When I had to [face the possibility of giving up soccer], I had to trust God and know that He was going to take care of everything. He gave me more than I could have wished for. The Olympics marked what would happen if I would trust Him.

"From that day on, I could see God doing incredible things through my soccer, so it's been my priority and my challenge to keep it that way. To keep soccer as His and not mine."

Q & A WITH MICHELLE AKERS

Q: *After the gold-medal game, the network covering the Games put you in charge of introducing the winning team. What was that like?*
Michelle Akers: I was certifiable—I didn't know what I was doing. It's funny to look at tapes of the postgame and see that I had so much energy. Before, when we were walking out to get our medals, I was lying on the ground waiting to go out. Then we walked out and got our medals. As we walked off and we got cornered for that interview, I just exploded with energy.

Q: *Where do you get your spiritual strength?*
Michelle: I wake up early each day and do a Bible study. Also, I enjoy working with either Bible Study Fellowship materials or doing the *Experiencing God* study. Also, I like to look into Charles Stanley's *In Touch*. Also, I have an advisory team that surrounds me—Christian friends who invest in me spiritually.

Q:: *What would you like to see happening in women's sports?*
Michelle: I'm learning that there are not very many outspoken female Christian athletes. That has been my new role. I'm used to

talking about sports and encouraging people, but being a spokesperson for Christ is something else! I'm working on getting women to be more outspoken. One of my dreams is to inspire more young Christian women athletes to speak out about their faith.

Q: *What advice do you have for young girls in sports?*
Michelle: First, I say, "Love it." It requires a lot to be the best you can be, so if you thoroughly love and enjoy that sport, you'll do what it takes to be prepared and to do your best. Second, go for it. A lot of kids and adults aren't willing to go for it 100 percent. You'll never find out if you can make it until you go for it 100 percent.

THE AKERS FILE

Additional information on Michelle Akers:
Standing Fast by Michelle Akers and Tim Nash
    JTC Sports, publisher; (919) 303-6611
Face to Face with Michelle Akers by Michelle Akers and
    Judith A. Nelson; Phone (800) 729-4351
Michelle Akers Website: http://www.michelleakers.com
Audio tape: "Ashes to Gold"; Phone (800) 653-8333

Rhonda Blades
WNBA Basketball Player
STRAIGHT SHOOTER

VITAL STATISTICS

Born: October 29, 1972, in Springfield, Missouri
Height: 5'7"
College: Graduated from Vanderbilt University; also holds graduate degree from Vanderbilt
Family: Husband, Parke Brown
Residence: Nashville, Tennessee
Special Interests: Rappelling, mountain biking, training/working out, working with children, friends

1992–95: Three-time Academic All-SEC
1993–94: First team SEC All-Tournament
1994–95: Honorable mention All-American
1994–95: Second team All-SEC
1995: Awarded an NCAA post-graduate scholarship

Led Vanderbilt in assists (4.2) as a senior
Vanderbilt's all-time leader in games played (132)
Second in career assists (505)
Member of Vanderbilt's 1,000-point club
Second all-time at Vanderbilt in three-pointers
Played in the 1993 NCAA Final Four
Made the first three-point basket in WNBA history

The WNBA may be relatively new, but its problems are as old as time. Rhonda Blades knows she has to be prepared for an environment that is sometimes hostile to her faith. "The pro environment is not really conducive to Christianity," she says. "You've got to be strong. It's very worldly, and there are a lot of temptations. I'm blessed with a family and a strong Christian husband, and we have a good church. I have a lot of people who love me unconditionally.

"My life revolves around my faith. I never want basketball to become an idol to me. Fortunately I have incredible friends who help me keep the proper perspective.'"

And whatever you do, whether in word or deed, do it all in the name of the Lord Jesus, giving thanks to God the Father through him (Colossians 3:17).
"That's probably my life verse. Whatever I do, I want to do it for God. Basketball opens a lot of doors. In the past year or so I've learned that basketball really makes me happy, but it really brings me a lot of joy when God uses my life to help others. To go out and

play hard and compete is not all I hope people notice. Most of all, I want them to see that I play to glorify God."

Rhonda Blades

Welcome to this afternoon's contest between the New York Liberty and the LA Sparks—the first game in WNBA history. About eight minutes are gone in the first half before a big crowd here at the Great Western Forum. Bringing the ball across the half-court line for the Liberty is their 5'7" point guard from Vanderbilt, Rhonda Blades. Blades passes off to her teammate Rebecca Lobo in the post. The Sparks double team lobo, and she kicks it out to Blades, who is behind the three-point arc. Blades gets the ball, goes up for a long jump shot—and SCORES! Rhonda Blades has just hit the first three-point shot in the history of the Women's National Basketball Association!"

The date was June 21, 1997, and the site was the Great Western Forum in Inglewood, California. With the NBC cameras rolling and the sports world tuning in to see what this sister league of the NBA was all about, Rhonda Blades made her indelible mark on the league in the first half of the inaugural game.

And an appropriate first impression it was for the Springfield, Missouri, native. It's not that Blades doesn't have other aspects of her game that would have been appropriate. She could have easily had the first steal or the first assist, since those are two outstanding parts of her game. But it seems most representative of who Rhonda Blades is to hit a long-range jumper—to prove that she is a straight shooter.

Both on the court and in her life, being honest and true are of utmost importance.

On the court, Blades has made a career out of making sure her shooting is true. Listen, for instance, to her explain her secret to long-range shooting. "You've got to shoot straight. The farther you go back, you still shoot the same shot you shoot from three feet away.

"You have to be straight, meaning your right foot, your right knee, your right hip, your right elbow, and your right wrist are all in a straight line. . . . It's a matter of shooting so much so that when I make a mistake, I know what I did wrong. So the next time I'm going to correct it. You only get to that point after you've got your shot straight."

Rhonda has developed her straight shooting technique through many years of hard work. She began playing basketball as a fourth grader back in Springfield, playing on a boys' club team. Each year after that, she was noticed by someone who moved her to the next level. "I always tried to play up, playing against older kids."

One example of that came when she was in junior high. She developed a friendship with Kelly Mago, who played for Southwest Missouri State University in Springfield. After Rhonda and Kelly met at a basketball camp, Kelly invited Rhonda to visit the college.

"Kelly would take me up to the college and let me play with the college girls, and I was only in junior high. I think girls that are younger need to see that it's not about beating your peers. It's about raising your level to somebody older than you. I would get the ball stolen occasionally, but you get to the point where you can handle it."

Also influencing Rhonda as a kid was her dad, a former star high school athlete in a town not far from Springfield. "My dad has probably been my biggest supporter," says Rhonda. "My mom is a more well-rounded supporter. But my dad has been big with basketball.

"My mom and dad were high school sweethearts. Mom was the cheerleader and the homecoming queen, and he was the star football player. But his best sport was track. I think he still has some records for the state. He was a sprinter. It was one of those small schools with six or seven people on the track team, yet they still won the state championship.

"We were just a boring middle-class family, but my parents spent all their money sending me to camps and stuff. And my dad built me a basketball court in our backyard. When a lot of people didn't think I could do it, he knew I could play pro one day. He was always there for me."

With that kind of support and with her natural drive, which she describes as manifesting itself in being "feisty" on the court, Blades worked her way up the basketball ladder. Her Parkview High School team went to the state Sweet Sixteen three out of the four years she was there. And her Amateur Athletic Union (AAU) team finished sixth in the nationals one year.

By the time she was a senior at Parkview, she was being recruited by colleges across the country. "I pretty much had my choice," she says. Among the many schools that wanted her, she narrowed her choice down to Vanderbilt, North Carolina State, and Northwestern—all schools with a reputation for academic excellence—before choosing Vanderbilt.

The Commodores got not only a young woman who could shoot a basketball straight from way downtown, but they also got a person who had a strong faith in Jesus Christ. Tony and Gail Blades had raised their two girls, Tonya and her younger sister Rhonda, in the Southland Community Church in Springfield. At age twelve, Rhonda was baptized. And the family was at church "twice on Sunday and once on Wednesday," as Rhonda describes it.

Yet when she arrived at Vanderbilt, Rhonda knew that she still had some growing to do spiritually. She began to just go through the motions. "I loved God and was a good kid, but I don't think I really desired the things of God until I went to college.

"I put basketball on a pedestal," she says. "As a freshman, I came in after having an incredible senior year, and I didn't play as much as I wanted. My coach knew he had me for the next four years, and the girl in front of me was a senior. He knew I was going to be the point guard for the next four years. So he molded me to make me what he wanted. It was frustrating. I was so worried about pleasing him all the time that I just didn't enjoy anything."

When summer vacation came around after her freshman year

at Vandy, Rhonda was ready for a break. She decided to return as a counselor to Kannakuk Kamp in Missouri, where she had been a camper two previous summers.

"That experience was freeing. It put everything into perspective for me. That's where I rededicated my life to the Lord. I decided that yes, loving God is really what I want to do."

With her new determination to love God, she went back to Vanderbilt for her sophomore season. It was a remarkable year for the Lady Commodores. Led by the awesome presence of 6'10" Heidi Gillingham, the Vanderbilt women spent much of the season ranked number one in the country. For her part, Blades became a more integral part of the team, increasing her stats considerably over the 1991–92 season. For instance, after firing just seventeen bombs from three-point range her freshman year, Rhonda launched ninety-six treys in her second year.

During the spring of 1993, the Lady Commodores accomplished what Rhonda still considers her career highlight when they made it to the NCAA Final Four at the Omni in Atlanta. Joining Iowa, Ohio State, and Texas Tech, Vanderbilt had a good shot at a national championship.

But then they ran into Sheryl Swoopes. In the semifinals against Vanderbilt, the Texas Tech superstar scored 31 points and grabbed 11 rebounds as Tech breezed past Vandy 60-46. Although Blades's team fell to the eventual champs (Tech beat Ohio State in the finals 84-82 behind Swoopes' 47-point performance), Rhonda still says, "Playing in the Final Four was phenomenal. I didn't understand it at the time, but what Sheryl Swoopes did was a turning point for women's college basketball. It was like that was the year women's basketball started. To be a part of that was unbelievable."

Another highlight for Blades came during her senior year. Four years earlier, when Rhonda was trying to decide which college to attend, she knew there was one place she couldn't go: Tennessee. The Volunteers, who have historically been the top program in women's college basketball, had just recruited another top point guard. Rhonda knew she didn't want to battle her for a spot on the team for four years, so she opted not to go there.

In her senior year, Blades and her teammates were up against

Tennessee in the SEC tournament. During her four years at Vanderbilt, Blades had not been on a team that had beaten Tennessee. It
was her last chance, and the Commodores beat the Vols. "We finally got over the hump," Rhonda says of the game that highlighted
her senior year.

During her career at Vanderbilt, Blades fired 471 three-pointers, for an average of more than three a game. "I was known as a
three-pointer shooter," she says. "Usually your point guard is not
one of your top options, so we went in most of the time to our big
people—especially Heidi. A lot of times they would double-team
her, collapse on her, and she would kick it out and I'd hit the three.
Or I'd come down and pull up for a three. The three-point shot is
probably the strongest point of my game."

At the time the excitement of her senior year of basketball was
being played out in Rhonda's life, another situation was develop-
ing that piqued her interest.

This new situation began quite a few months earlier when
Donna, Rhonda's college roommate, and another acquaintance
named Buddy began to tell Rhonda that there was a guy she
should meet. His name was Parke Brown. His name, which Rhonda thought unusual, stuck with her. Parke was a Baylor graduate
who was living in Nashville, home of Vanderbilt.

Later, Donna asked Buddy to see if Parke would lend her his
truck to help move some things—both hoping to get Parke and
Rhonda together. But when the day came and Parke parked his
truck at the girls' apartment, Rhonda was gone. Donna and
Buddy's matchmaking wasn't going very well.

Later, Donna, who was working with some inner-city youth,
asked if Rhonda could come to a basketball outreach she was helping set up. Despite the fact that she had a huge test the next day,
Rhonda went to the event. Conveniently, Parke was also there. "We
met," Rhonda recalls, "but I was kind of out of it, thinking about
my test. I hardly even remembered him."

But Donna wouldn't let her forget him. A few months after
the basketball outreach, Buddy helped Donna and Rhonda find a
new apartment. To thank him, they invited him over for dinner.
Then Buddy, as Rhonda puts it, "slyly conned Parke into having
Parke meet Buddy at my apartment."

This time, there were no excuses for Rhonda not to pay better attention to Parke. "We hit it off immediately," Rhonda says. Well, perhaps it can't be called "immediately," since it had been six months since Buddy and Donna had tried to get them together.

"He had this wonderful personality," Rhonda says. "He's very outgoing and friendly. We went together for a year and a half."

When Rhonda's career at Vanderbilt was over, she had several options. She could take her post-grad scholarship and get a master's degree. She could concentrate on her new, growing relationship with Parke. She could begin work as a nurse practitioner. She could play pro basketball.

Which option did she choose? All of them.

In the fall of 1995, Rhonda began graduate studies. Soon after school started, Parke and Rhonda were out doing one of their favorite outdoor activities—rappelling off a 100-foot cliff in Foster Falls, Tennessee—when Parke asked Rhonda for her hand. Not to help him down the cliff, but in marriage. She said yes, and they began their rapid climb toward the wedding.

"We had a two-month engagement. I planned a wedding in the middle of grad school." In December 1995 they were married.

Parke, who owns his own business in Nashville, was just the kind of man Rhonda was looking for: someone like her dad. "The one thing I wanted was a spiritual leader," she says. "That's hard to find. He has such a servant's heart, and that's rare. A lot of friends who are married, it seems like they are dragging their husbands. God calls men to lead the house. I'd do anything for my husband out of my love for him. It's easy to submit when he loves you like God wants him to. Our love is reciprocal."

As she was finishing her graduate degree as a new bride in 1996, a new development cropped up. The American Basketball League was just getting started, and the league was conducting tryout camps for women who wanted to give it a shot.

"I thought, *I have this opportunity; I might as well go for it,*" Blades says. "I'm 5'7". I'm known for being in really good shape. Athletically, I'm not going to kill you, but endurance-wise, with fundamentals, and by outsmarting you, that's pretty much my game."

But Blades had a couple of strikes against her as she went to the camps. First, with her job and her graduate school studies and her new marriage, she didn't have sufficient time to train. "I was at about 70 or 75 percent in shape."

Second, she didn't have name recognition. "You've got to know some people who are going to plug you. For all anybody knew, I had quit playing basketball."

"I went to the tryouts and continued to make the draft pool list. Then, on the third day, the ABL brought in the people they wanted most. Still, I made it to the final group that would be drafted, but I just didn't get drafted initally. I was later drafted by the Colorado Xplosion, but opted to wait for the WNBA.

"It was a good experience because I proved that I could play with the people in that league. It really worked out for the best. I needed to finish my schooling, which Vanderbilt was paying for, and I didn't need anything to get in my way."

Blades finished graduate school and began working in her selected field.

"Then the WNBA thing came up, and I got invited to their draft camp. I went there and was selected by New York as their ninth pick.

"It was a big thrill to be selected, but I thought I might go earlier. I made the draft pool and then most teams drafted post players. It was like they decided that point guards weren't that important. I think that might have come back to hurt a few of the teams.

"I've been patient," she says about the entire selection procedure. "If I've learned anything from this, it's patience, and that God is in control. I actually have no control over anything."

Except, of course, shooting straight. Which brings us back to Blades's first year in the WNBA. Besides hitting that inaugural trey, Rhonda contends that she remembers a couple of other games with fondness.

One was on July 23 when the Liberty visited Charlotte for an Eastern Conference showdown. The Sting had been very tough at home, and New York was eager to shut them down at the Hive. With Rhonda's family in the stands, she had one of her best games, picking up a couple of steals, hitting all of her shots, and helping the Liberty beat the Sting 65-63.

"It's hard to contribute when you're a backup. You're in there to give people a rest and to build on a lead. Anything extra you do is a bonus. I felt like I contributed that game. That was an exciting game."

Another highlight came on the final day of the short WNBA season in 1997. The Liberty was in Houston to play the Comets for the first WNBA championship. To get there, New York had defeated Phoenix 59–41 and Houston had taken Charlotte down 70-54.

On August 30, a sellout crowd of 16,285 was on hand at the Summit in Houston to catch the action. Looking back, Blades said she knew the Liberty was in trouble. "Houston was at home, and they were ready for us. We had beaten them three times at home. But now they were out for blood, and we were tired."

Behind league and championship MVP Cynthia Cooper, the Comets blazed past the Liberty 65 to 51 and laid claim to the title trophy and first-year bragging rights. Blades played thirteen minutes in the final game and had two assists for her efforts.

"I really enjoyed getting to the championship. You hate to go and lose, but it's unfortunate that it was a one-game series," Blades says in reflection. "But they were definitely the better team that day."

As Rhonda reflects further on that first year in the surprisingly popular WNBA, she has an admirable attitude toward what took place in a season that seemed to come and go in a flash. "It was nuts. Every day, something incredible happened. It was so fast. Just now am I beginning to just enjoy it and say, 'You know, that was really neat.'

"Even though you want to be the [big stars like] Teresa Weatherspoon and the Rebecca Lobo, that wasn't my role. I really got to enjoy it. I didn't have to deal with the media. Not that that's bad, but I really got to just play basketball. And for me, that's why I'm there. I'm in the WNBA to meet the kids and influence them and be a light for God. That's what I got to do and I got paid for it."

When that first season ended, Rhonda went back home to Nashville, where she and Parke are active in their church, participating in Bible studies. He continues to run his business, and Rhonda has gone back to work in nursing. On the side, she teaches private basketball lessons to young WNBA wannabes.

In this new world of women in professional basketball, it's a bit of a throwback to the old days of men's basketball when the players finished their seasons and went back to a normal life—working and blending into the community. For Rhonda Blades, that is perfectly all right. She's not in it for glory and riches and fame.

She just loves basketball and wants to use it as a way to reach people with the gospel.

What else would you expect from such a straight shooter?

Q & A WITH RHONDA BLADES

Q: *What sports figure do you admire the most?*
Rhonda Blades: Dean Smith is my all-time favorite coach in the world. He always ran a class program. He got it done the right way. Honestly, I think part of his retirement was that the state of college athletics isn't the best, and I don't think he wanted to compromise his standards in any way. That shows me even more that he's a man of integrity.

Q: *How did you develop such an accurate shot?*
Rhonda: I was one of those kids who watched a lot of TV and watched a lot of people shoot. If you go to camps, you get the basics. Then every summer, I'd try to correct something. One summer, I moved my shot from the hip to the shoulder. The next summer I worked on getting my left hand out of the shot.

When I was at Vanderbilt, we had a guy named Buzz Braman. He used to be the shooting coach for Shaquille O'Neal. Coach [Jim] Foster always brought him in to do shooting clinics with us. One summer I went and worked his clinic. He broke it down into four steps. It really is a basic thing. We make it really difficult. I learned from him the fine-tuning points of shooting.

Q: *How do you handle the pressures of pro basketball?*
Rhonda: One of my favorite verses is 1 Peter 5:7, which says, "Cast all your cares on Him, for He cares for you." I think in everything we do, whether it's basketball or family or relationships or job or anything, we're always anxious. For me, I have to give it all to God,

or I'll drive myself crazy. With playing in a game, this helps with confidence. I don't have to worry about anything. Just give it to God. He's going to use me the way He's going to use me.

Q: *Because of your status as a player in the inaugural WNBA season, do you see yourself as a pioneer in women's basketball?*
Rhonda: It's hard for me to see myself as a pioneer. I'm friends with Nancy Lieberman-Cline, and Carol Blazejowski was my GM [general manager], and these women are already in the Hall of Fame. It's hard for me to think of myself as a pioneer, when the credit needs to go to them. There are so many women who've been playing basketball over the years that most people have never heard about. These women have many incredible stories that few people have heard. I've walked into a great time for women, but the thanks needs to go to the women before me. If it wasn't for them, we wouldn't be where we are today.

THE BLADES FILE

Year One: New York Liberty

		Field Goals			3-point FG		Free Throws					
G	Min	FG/FGA	Pct.	FG/FGA	Pct.		FT/FTA	Pct.	Steals	Assists	Points
28	290	25 70	.357	17 54	.315		13 20	.650	14	30	80

Ruthie Bolton-Holifield

WNBA Basketball Player

ALL IN THE FAMILY

VITAL STATISTICS

Born: May 27, 1967, in Lucedale, Mississippi
Height: 5'9"
College: Auburn (Exercise physiology)
Family: Husband, Mark Holifield
Residence: Gainesville, Florida
Special Interests: Family, gospel music, writing in her diary

CAREER HONORS

1986: US Olympic Festival gold medal
1988, 1989: Named to the NCAA Mideast Region All-Tournament teams; also named to the SEC All-Academic teams
1988: Named to the NCAA Final Four All-Tournament team
1989: All-SEC second team
1991: USA Basketball Female Athlete of the Year
1991: First American woman to play professionally in Hungary
1994: Goodwill Games gold medal
1996: Olympic gold medal
1997: All-WNBA first team

OTHER HIGHLIGHTS

Played professionally in Europe: Italy, 1992–94; Hungary, 1991–92; Sweden, 1990–91
Finished third in MVP voting in WNBA, 1997
Sang in an Italian group called Antidum Tarantula while playing overseas
Named first-ever WNBA Player of the Week after the initial week of play in the league in 1997

WARMING UP

Soon after the WNBA season ended its first campaign, the league announced that a group of its top players was going to Europe to take on a couple of top teams—one in Germany and one in Italy—before making an appearance at the McDonald's Championship in Paris. As Ruthie Bolton prepared to take this trip, which for her was a return to her professional roots, she spoke of another type of exhibition basketball series she would like to be involved with someday. "I've thought about playing with Athletes in Action," a touring team of Christian players who play college teams and seek opportunities to discuss Christ. "I would really enjoy a chance to travel with them and share my faith that way." For a woman who has done just about everything else in basketball, it does seem like a great opportunity to consider.

Who shall separate us from the love of Christ? Shall trouble or hardship or persecution or famine or nakedness or danger or sword? . . . No, in all these things we are more than conquerors through him who loved us. For I am convinced that neither death nor life, neither angels nor demons, neither the present nor the future, nor any powers, neither height nor depth, nor anything else in all creation, will be able to separate us from the love of God that is in Christ Jesus our Lord (Romans 8:35–39).

Ruthie says, "No matter what happens, no one has the control to take me from God's love. Knowing that is an assurance I need."

Ruthie Bolton-Holifield

I f you've paid attention at all to the women's basketball scene in the past several years, you could not have missed the name Ruthie Bolton (or Bolton-Holifield).

She was, for instance, a key member of the USA Basketball team that barnstormed the world in the months before the 1996 Olympics, taking on and defeating every challenger. Once they had swept past the Brazilians 111-87 to capture the championship in Atlanta, the team had easily earned the title Best Women's Basketball Team on the Planet. The victory over Brazil gave the women a perfect 60-0 record under the coaching of Tara VanDerveer.

So, you probably know the name Ruthie Bolton. But you probably don't know the name of another Bolton basketball prodigy—the one who actually possesses the gold medal that was awarded on the podium at Atlanta. That gold medal belongs to Mae Ola Bolton, Ruthie's sister.

Confused? All you need to know to understand why Mae Ola and not Ruthie has the gold is this: Family is everything to Ruthie.

Many athletes are influenced and encouraged by their families, but for Ruthie Bolton, a lot more was going on than that. Her unique family in McClain, Mississippi, gave her something not many other families can give: scrimmages.

As Alice Ruth Bolton was growing up in McClain, she was one of twenty children of Rev. Linwood and Leola Bolton. If there ever was a self-sufficient family, it was the Bolton Gang.

For one thing, they met many of their needs by growing their own food. "We had many acres of gardens we planted," says Ruthie. "We got our peas and corn and greens from there, and at harvest time we would freeze them. We would live on that all the time. We never went without."

Also, the family had a built-in spiritual mentor in Dad. A minister in local churches, Rev. Bolton made sure things were first taken care of at home. His instruction in matters of the Spirit paid off for Ruthie as a young girl. "I was saved when I was seven," she says. Five of Ruthie's brothers are now preachers, and the family has also created two gospel music CDs.

Having a houseful of brothers and sisters also meant that there was never a shortage of competition. "We did a lot more than kids do now. They sit around watching TV and playing computers. We were always outside. We made up games. We jumped fences; we had relay games. And we played basketball. That was the game a lot of people could play. Ten people could play at a time. We had so many people around, it was something we did a lot of the time."

Introduced to basketball by the sheer convenience of having a sport that could occupy half the Bolton brood, Ruthie learned to love it. "I think I did it because I enjoyed it. Knowing me, if I had had access to tennis, I might have been a tennis player. I really don't know. Basketball was just the thing I had access to."

It also helped that the family had some natural athleticism. Besides Ruthie, others who took their skills out of McClain were Nathaniel, who has played in the World League of American Football; Inez, who played hoops for the University of Florida; and Mae Ola, who preceded Ruthie on the basketball courts of Auburn.

Adding to the basketball influence in Ruthie's family was her brother James. "Once I realized that I might be able to play in college, James started working with me. He helped me before I went to college and while I was in college."

All in all, the Bolton family had a lot going for it. Looking back on it, Ruthie is filled with appreciation. "I wouldn't take anything to replace the life my parents made for us. We never went without. We lived in a decent house. My mom always got us what we needed. We may not have had Calvin Kleins when they first came out, but we always had jeans. My parents did an excellent job of making sure we had what we needed."

And it wasn't just clothes and food that Linwood and Leola provided. "It was special. At the time, I probably didn't appreciate it the way I should. But I look back on it now, and I thank God for times when my dad said no when I wanted him to say yes when we wanted to go certain places. Dad knew better. I look back on it now, and I look at the people who were allowed to do those things. They are nowhere but in McClain. They haven't advanced; they haven't excelled. So every time I go home, I just want to thank my dad for the discipline and the guidelines he gave us."

In fact, Ruthie makes no apologies for saying that her dad is the person she most admires in life. She says he "sets a good example and practices what he preaches."

Yet it was to her sister Mae Ola that Ruthie presented her gold medal. It was to her basketball-playing older sibling that she bestowed the most important earthly award she will ever earn.

Why?

As Ruthie was beginning to make her mark on the McClain High School basketball program in the early '80s, Mae Ola was trailblazing the way. She seemed to be the one headed for basketball greatness. And indeed after a successful high school career, she enrolled at Auburn, where she continued to excel.

Ruthie, on the other hand, was told when she went to Auburn that she couldn't play at that level. "I wanted to prove everybody wrong," she says. For three years, the sisters played together on the Tigers squad. They were both selected to play in the 1986 US Olympic Festival and in the World University Games in 1990.

For Mae Ola, though, 1988 was the year of decision. Because of her standout career at Auburn, the next logical step was the Olympics. However, she failed to make the team at the Olympic trials. From 1989 through 1991, Mae Ola took her skills to Europe, where she played in Spain and Italy.

In the meantime, Ruthie continued her own hoops excursion. After Auburn, she played overseas for several years and represented the United States in various world competitions, culminating in her selection to the 1996 US Olympic team.

So, when Ruthie earned that coveted metallic disc hanging from a ribbon on Day 17 of the 1996 Olympics in Atlanta, she knew what she was going to do with it. She gave it to Mae Ola, her sister who had paved the way for her at Auburn and who, Ruthie says, "should have played in the Olympics. It was her dream too. I thought Mae Ola would be where I am today—still playing."

What was it about Ruthie Bolton that kept her going? What spurred her on? It's a combination of things she has learned— lessons picked up in McClain from James and other Boltons, lessons given to her by former Auburn assistant coach Carol Ross, lessons provided by Mae Ola, and lessons learned through that grueling yet rewarding year of playing for USA Basketball.

As Ruthie reflects on the accomplishments of the Olympic team, she says what they did can be summed up in one word: "Commitment."

"Tara [VanDerveer] pointed us to a task. She wanted to separate the women from the girls. She brought out the best in all of us. Even though it was tough, she pushed us to play at another level, and that's how you win championships. You have to elevate to the level that is needed.

"My main goal was to prepare well. I knew that once we got to the Olympics, the winning would take care of itself. When you develop a habit, you can play by instinct. If you're working on good habits, then those habits become instincts. And that's what Tara made sure we did. She made sure we practiced more on good habits than bad habits. To me the Olympics was easy. We had already fought the war and won."

Bolton had won many big games in her career. Her high school team won the state championship twice. She had captured gold medals in the Goodwill Games, in Olympic Festivals, and at the World University Games. But nothing came close to what she experienced in Atlanta.

"It's a memory I will always cherish," she says. "It's the ultimate in basketball. No matter how many championships you win, there's nothing like winning an Olympic gold medal for your country."

And there's nothing like giving it to your sister as a gesture of love and respect.

The women of USA Basketball may have claimed "the ultimate in basketball" as Bolton described it, but they were not finished making history. They, plus many other top female basketball players, were about to embark on something experimental. Something whose time, it seemed, had come. Professional women's basketball.

It had been tried before. Several leagues had come and gone over the past fifteen years or so, but this was a different era. This was an era during which college women's teams were filling arenas. An era that included the highly successful USA Basketball schedule. An era of some well-known women's players.

So, in the fall of 1996, the American Basketball League kicked off its schedule. Among the players in that league were several Olympic gold medalists. Ruthie Bolton was not among them. On November 21, 1996, the rival Women's National Basketball Association announced that she had signed to play during their summer season in 1997.

The grand experiment of the two professional leagues was under way, and Bolton had decided to go with the league that was started by the NBA. She was assigned to the Sacramento Monarchs. To tune up for her domestic professional debut, Ruthie went back overseas and played for Galatsaray in Turkey.

It was her fourth European team and her fifth time to play on the continent. She had discovered in her earlier excursions across the Atlantic to play ball that the times over there were periods of spiritual growth as well, and she hoped this would be no different.

"Playing in Europe—that taught me a lot," she says. "It matured me in a lot of ways. It made me wiser, because I had to adjust to a whole new culture. . . . I had to worship God and do my Bible study at home because I wasn't able to go to church. It definitely made me stronger in many, many ways.

"I've been fortunate enough to have many experiences that other people haven't had. The good and the bad experiences have helped me. I'm glad I went overseas to play because it does something to you mentally, and it makes you a strong person. You don't have everything handed to you like in America, where everything is so easy. Over there, you really have to make adjustments, and that's what makes a person wiser. I came through it, and I'm glad I did it."

In her final trip to play overseas before starting her WNBA

career, one of the problems was that the team faced some financial problems, forcing Ruthie to return to the United States before the Turkish season was over.

When the WNBA season tipped off on June 21, though, Bolton didn't seem to be hurt by the loss of playing time in Europe. She immediately established herself as one of the top players in the league. In her first two games for the Monarchs, Bolton recorded double-doubles. In the opener, against the Utah Starzz, she scored eighteen points and grabbed eleven rebounds. Two days later against the New York Liberty, she fired home twenty-seven points and picked up twelve rebounds. After her first two games in this new league, she was second in the league in scoring and rebounds, first in the WNBA in steals per game (5), and third in the league in minutes played (36.5).

This league seemed to be just the right fit for thirty-year-old Ruthie Bolton.

- Throughout the season, she reached several milestones. On July 2, she became the first WNBA player to reach 100 points when she scored 20 points against Utah.
- After the first third of the season, Ruthie was leading the league in scoring with a 21.1 points per game (PPG) average.
- A midseason knee injury took her out of action for a few games, but when she returned, she was hot. She says one of her highlights from her first year was a series of four games after she returned from the injury—games in which she scored 28, 25, 34, and 34 points. That first 34-point performance marked just the second time a WNBA player had hit for more than 30 points in a game.
- Bolton finished the year with a 19.4 PPG average, second only to league MVP Cynthia Cooper's 22.2.

The first season was by no means all good news. Bolton's team finished with a 10-18 win-loss record, finishing a disappointing third in the Western Conference. The injury robbed Ruthie of any chance to win some of the statistical awards a full season may have given her. And after those four stellar games in which she scored 121 points, an average of 30 points per game, Ruthie finished with some mediocre performances.

Yet she is not afraid to count that first season as a success. "I knew the WNBA would do well, and to be one of the premier players was a great experience. My team didn't do that well, but to see the fan attendance that we had and the accomplishments we had as a league was encouraging. I think, most of all, we were able just to have fun.

"I can look back and say I had a great time playing pro basketball because it was something I did by choice. It shouldn't be miserable; a player should enjoy it. I definitely reached my goal by having fun."

And when it was all over, the league named her third in balloting for Most Valuable Player and voted her to the league All-WNBA team. That was gratifying. "My most memorable experience was when I was announced to the All-WNBA first team. That's something I really wanted. Since my team didn't do well, I wanted something to represent the Monarchs."

Ruthie Bolton not only represented the Monarchs and the WNBA well during her maiden season in the league, she also represented her family well. It's something the Boltons of McClain have been doing for a long time.

One of the reasons Ruthie can do that so well is because of some spiritual advice someone gave her one time. She doesn't recall who told her, but she says it has made all the difference for her.

"Life is full of decisions. We have a tendency to worry about the many small things that make life an emergency. Small stuff that we worry about unnecessarily. But if you look a year from now, will this really matter? Also, sometimes you think about whether to do things that your conscience tells you are not right. Something that really helps me out is knowing that with everything I do in life, I think: *Everything you do will pass, but only what's done for Christ will last.* That really helps with those decisions."

In McClain, Mississippi, Linwood Bolton would smile with gratitude to hear his little girl Ruthie say that. That's exactly the kind of thing he and his late wife Leola tried to teach their children.

Too bad Ruthie doesn't have another gold medal to give him.

Q & A WITH RUTHIE BOLTON-HOLIFIELD

Q: *You have good stats in scoring, steals, and even rebounds. What is the strongest part of your game?*

Ruthie Bolton-Holifield: I think my game is really balanced. I think in the WNBA I've improved on my passing—getting the ball to open people. And I think something I need to work on more is mixing my game up. Shooting from the outside, penetrating, pulling up. I need to penetrate and get to the line. I didn't get to the line enough. I need to penetrate and draw more fouls.

Q: *How did you and your husband, Mark, meet?*

Ruthie: After my last year at Auburn, I was taking summer school. I had just finished my finals that summer, and I was ready to go to play ball overseas, in Sweden. I was up late packing, getting ready to go home. I went to the store to get something I needed. He was a deputy sheriff, and he stopped by the store to check on the lady who worked at the store, and that's when I met him. He recognized me, and we started talking about basketball. That was June. We were engaged in November. We got married in 1990.

Q: *What do you try to do to grow spiritually?*

Ruthie: I don't get to go to church as much as I'd like to because of my schedule. When I get a chance, I go hear one of my brothers preach. Also, I listen to tapes of my father and brothers. I like to read the Bible and do my own meditation. I read other books besides the Bible. I read inspirational books, but not just the Bible. . . . Also, I like gospel music. My brothers have a CD, and I like to listen to them a lot.

Q: *What kind of advice do you give to young girls who see you as an athletic role model?*

Ruthie: I tell them: I think you have to really believe in yourself as an athlete. You have to set goals and believe that you can achieve those goals. Then do whatever it takes to achieve those goals. If you set goals, and you don't achieve them, it's because you didn't want to. Don't let other people discourage you from reaching your goals.

I've always had to exceed what other people thought of me. I'm still doing it every day, exceeding expectations. So stay positive, keeping the positive mental attitude, which is something my father taught me. You're in control of your actions and the way you react to a situation. Never give up, and stay committed. Set goals, work toward your goals, keep a positive attitude, and be willing to sacrifice whatever it takes to reach your goal.

THE BOLTON FILE

Year	Games	FG/FGA	Pct.	FT/FTA	Pct.	Ast	Steals	Points/Avg
1985–89 Auburn	132	530–1038	.511	108–157	.688	536	246	1176/8.9
1996 Olympics	8	21–24	.447	15–21	.714	16	23	102/12.8
1997 WNBA	23	164–408	.402	53–69	.768	59	54	447/19.4

Amanda Borden

1996 Olympic Gold Medalist: Gymnastics
THE CINCINNATI KID

VITAL STATISTICS

Born: May 10, 1977, in Cincinnati, Ohio
Height: 5'2"
Single
Residence: Cincinnati, Ohio
Special Interests: Bicycling, reading, shopping, computers

1992: McDonald's American Cup, eighth place
1992: Olympic trials, seventh place
1993: Tokyo Cup, third place, uneven bars
1996: Gold medal, gymnastics

WARMING UP

For more than a year after Amanda and her six teammates on the US Olympic team captured the gold medal and America's heart, she was still touring with her friends—performing exhibitions in cities across the land. Amanda is still in awe of the opportunity. "I'm just ecstatic that I get a chance to do that. I love to do the Tour. I love to perform. And to be paid for that is like an honor." That's a refreshing attitude when guys her age are demanding millions and millions of dollars to play their sport—sometimes with far fewer credentials than Amanda and her friends have.

FAVORITE BIBLE PASSAGE

I can do everything through him who gives me strength (Philippians 4:13).

At the Cincinnati Gymnastics Academy, where Amanda Borden has trained for years, the coach, Mary Lee Tracy, chooses a saying each year as a theme. When Amanda first came under Tracy's teaching, the theme for the year was Philippians 4:13. "I liked that," says Amanda. "You don't have control over what is going to happen, so you have to have faith in God that things will turn out all right."

Amanda Borden

Perhaps the most important career move Amanda Borden ever made was being born in Cincinnati. She could actually have been born anywhere, but the important thing was that after Amanda was born, when Doug and Patty Borden took her home from the hospital, they were living in the Queen City. The family had no inkling in 1977 how vital their hometown connections would someday be for their little girl.

Like any other active youngster growing up in the shadow of Riverfront Stadium and the Big Red Machine, Amanda took up T-ball as one of her original sports. When she discovered that there were a couple of minor flaws in her game—namely she couldn't hit or catch the ball—she moved from the diamond to the soccer field.

That lasted until she began losing interest when she didn't have the ball.

By this time, it was 1984, an Olympic year. As Amanda and her family watched the Los Angeles Olympics on TV, a teenager from Fairmont, West Virginia, just a four-hour drive from Cincinnati, was stealing America's heart with her remarkable gymnastic skills and her pixie personality.

Seven-year-old Amanda Borden was enthralled with Mary Lou Retton. If T-ball didn't work out and soccer was a bust, then perhaps it was time for her to move on to Mary Lou's sport.

Soon Amanda was in the gym. She wasn't seeking Olympic

glory. She just thought it looked like fun. At this point, whether she lived in Cincinnati or Paducah or Terre Haute didn't matter. For beginners, there is always a place to go to learn the basics of gymnastics.

As a beginner, though, Amanda was impressive. At first, her mom signed her up for a one-hour-a-week lesson. Immediately, the coaches saw something special in her and moved her up to a higher level. Soon she was in the gym six hours a week.

Amanda progressed so rapidly that before she was ten, she was selected to travel to Tennessee for a week of elite training. Whatever that week taught her about gymnastics, it taught her more about herself. She didn't like being away from home—at least without her family. She was a Cincinnati kid at heart.

As her skill increased and her need to compete grew, Amanda began to travel throughout Ohio, Kentucky, Indiana, and Michigan. For those excursions, Doug and Patty packed up the family vehicle, brought along a friend to keep Amanda's brother Bryan company, and made a family trip out of it.

For Amanda, it was as important to be with her family as it was to compete. Which brings us back to the importance of their living in Cincinnati. When Amanda was thirteen, it was time for her to get some world-class training. It was time—if she intended to achieve the highest level of gymnastic achievement—to find a coach who could take her from her level all the way to the top.

For many young gymnasts, that watershed time in their lives means a forced separation from the family. It means moving to a city far from home and living with another family while training. It means uprooting from home at one of life's most vulnerable, tender times.

But for Amanda Borden, all it meant was a twenty-minute drive from Finneytown to Fairfield. In Fairfield was the Cincinnati Gymnastics Academy, whose coach, Mary Lee Tracy, was one of those world-class mentors that young gymnastics stars seek out. Amanda didn't have to leave home to pursue her dream.

"Our family was always really close," Amanda says. "And that was always really important to me. I would never have moved away from my family to train."

Although the Bordens didn't have to split up for Amanda to

train, there were enough sacrifices to go around. As Amanda thinks back on the regimen she had to keep, she thinks her brother Bryan may have gotten the worst end of the deal. He had to give up a lot of his time as the family traveled around following Amanda's budding career. "My brother sacrificed a lot growing up," she says. "I remember when I made the Olympic team at the trials, I looked up into the stands and saw my brother, who is pretty quiet and not very emotional. My parents were laughing and crying and clapping, and my brother was standing up and cheering. It meant so much to me to know that I had his support."

As the family made their collective trek through Amanda's athletic pursuits, there were high times (like the 1996 selection to the team), and there were definitely low times. One of those low times came in 1991.

Amanda was just fourteen years old, but she was competing near the top of the elite level. Things seemed to be on track toward the Olympic trials in 1992. As Amanda trained for the USA Championships, however, she was in the middle of a tumbling routine when she heard her arm make a popping sound. "I didn't hyperextend it or anything," she recalls. "It just made a funny sound. Then it really hurt." When she checked it out with a doctor, she was shocked to hear him say, "Your elbow is broken." That would keep Amanda off the practice floor for at least six weeks.

Finally, she was cleared to resume training. Not long after that, she was doing a leap as she practiced a routine and she felt something pop in her leg. It was a hamstring.

Suddenly, Amanda's bright gymnastics prospects looked bleak. The USA Championships were out of the picture now. Could she get herself back in shape for the Olympic trials the following year? Did she even want to try?

At first, her answer was no. Amanda was ready to quit at age fourteen.

And that's what she did. She told her parents that she was quitting gymnastics.

Doug and Patty had invested seven years in their daughter's gymnastics. They had paid the fees, shelled out for lessons, hauled Amanda around the Midwest, given up their free time. And she was quitting. Many parents would have trouble containing their anger at such a decision. Many would insist that their child must continue.

Not the Bordens. "My parents didn't pressure me," she says. "They let me make my decision."

Within three days, Amanda was back in the gym, working as hard as ever to get herself ready for 1992. She decided on her own that quitting was not the answer.

"My parents never pushed me," she says. "I can't imagine going to the gym every day and being unhappy—doing it because my parents pressured me. If I would have stayed in because my parents pushed me, I wouldn't have been happy. If they had, I wouldn't have made the Olympics."

As a matter of fact, she didn't. At least not the first time.

After resuming training, Amanda returned to top form and went into the US Championships in great shape. At that event, competing against the best women in America, Borden finished fifth—good enough to qualify her for the Olympic trials. It looked like the homebody from Cincinnati had a good chance of taking a trip to Barcelona.

The 1992 Olympic trials couldn't have gone better for Amanda. Although she was not among the top finishers, she did finish seventh among the women seeking to qualify. And as anyone who recalls the name Magnificent 7 knows, that's the magic number. The team consists of seven members.

Not so fast. Don't pack that bag just yet. The US gymnastics officials had something else in mind. Two other women, who were injured and could not compete in the trials, were selected for the sixth and seventh spots on the team. Amanda and Kim Kelly (the sixth-best finisher) were not going to Barcelona.

Thinking back on that major disappointment, Amanda says, "At first, it wasn't a big deal. I had tried my best, and that's all I could do. But as time went by, I realized that only seven girls make the Olympic team every four years. I realized I should have been there. I deserved to go. I made the team, and then somebody took my dream away.

"I went through a really tough time. I didn't know if I could hang in there until 1996. I didn't know if I wanted to. I didn't know if I wanted to work that hard anymore. And it was really tough on my parents. They saw how hard I worked, and I go out there and somebody else takes it away from me. It's really tough for parents."

One thing stuck in Amanda's mind, though, as she contemplated her future in light of the disappointment of 1992. It came in part from the teaching of Coach Tracy and in part from her own faith. "We know that whatever happens is in God's plan. You work as hard as you can, and then leave the results to Him."

For her part, Amanda's mom looks back on that 1992 experience with the same optimism. "You just have to believe that God's timing is right," says Patty Borden. "God had a wonderful plan for her. It was so much greater in 1996 than it would have been in 1992."

As Amanda began preparing for the next four years of competition, she had some help at the Cincinnati Gymnastics Company. Jaycie Phelps, another elite athlete, moved to Cincinnati to train with Amanda under Mary Lee Tracy. Jaycie's arrival was a huge boost to Amanda.

"I feel like if I didn't have Jaycie to train with, I wouldn't have hung around until 1996. In 1992, I trained by myself, and it was very tough going into the gym every day. Working out with Mary Lee was great, but it made a big difference to have a teammate who was going through the same things I was. She was always there for me when I felt like I couldn't go any further."

Together, the three of them formed a bond around gymnastics and their shared faith. Tracy, who uses her gymnastics expertise as a way to witness to young gymnasts about her faith in Jesus Christ, spent many hours in Bible study and prayer with Amanda and Jaycie.

"Before every competition, Jaycie, Mary Lee, and I always pray. It's not to win or beat anyone. It's just to go out and stay safe and to have a great competition and have fun. We know that whatever happens was meant to be at that point in our lives. That usually calms us. We realize that the results aren't really in our hands anymore. They're in God's hands. We know that whatever happens is in God's plan. That's how we approach competition."

Between 1992 and 1996, Amanda continued to improve her standing among US gymnastics. In 1993, she finished fourth in the USA Championships, and in 1994 she finished third. At the Pan

American Games she captured two gold medals and two silvers while serving as the team captain. Atlanta was beginning to look like a real possibility.

The 1995 gymnastic season was less promising. Again injuries slowed Amanda's progress. This time a broken toe and twisted ankle were the culprits, keeping her out of some of the top competitions of the year. The bad streak continued into 1996 when she broke a bone in her hand just months before the Olympic trials were to be held. But by mid-March she was back into full-time training.

By June 30, she was an Olympian. Unlike the 1992 trials, nothing would stop her from making the elite seven. Not even nervousness.

"At the trials, the nerves are incredible. You've trained for twelve or thirteen years and it all comes down to one day. For me, there's more pressure there than at the Olympics. I knew that I was going to be on the bottom half of the team, which was fine, and I knew I would be fighting for the last couple of spots. The pressure right there was pretty tough. But knowing that I had worked as hard as I could and that I couldn't have done anything else to help myself gave me confidence. I also knew whatever happened, it would be God's will."

What happened was that both Amanda and her training partner Jaycie made the team. And Amanda was named team captain.

The pressure may have been greater in Boston at the trials, but nothing could prepare Amanda and her teammates for the emotions they would feel a few weeks later in Atlanta.

"I remember walking into the Georgia Dome for the first time," Amanda says, "and it was just for podium training, which was practice. We had about 25,000 people there just to watch practice. Any time the crowd saw an American team walking out, they just went crazy."

That was just practice. What came next was even more remarkable. "As captain, I was the leader of the line. I remember the first day of competition, I walked out and there were 40,000 people in the stands. It felt like every one of them was pulling for the United States. I remember that I had a big lump in my throat, and I had to fight back the tears because I couldn't believe that I was in the

Olympics and all these people were so proud of us. They wanted us to do great.

"I knew if I started crying then, it probably would be tough to pull back into form for the competition. We had to go out there really tough, basically with no emotions. We were out there to compete and do our gymnastics, not to play around or cry or do those kinds of things.

"I'm a very emotional person, so I had to fight it very hard when I walked out not to cry. I don't know if I'll ever have that feeling again."

The emotions, of course, would not peak for these young women as they walked to their competition. The real heart tug came later in one of the most dramatic finishes in Olympic history. In a scene no movie writer would imagine, Borden's teammate Kerry Strug landed her vault on a damaged leg to assure the US women of the gold medal. As she hit the mat, the Georgia Dome erupted in thunderous ecstasy. The Magnificent 7 was born, and now the emotions could flow freely.

"I had so many different emotions in Atlanta it's pretty hard to remember what it felt like," Amanda says. "I remember knowing that we had won, but I wasn't going to believe it until we were up on the awards stand getting our medals. I don't think that when it was happening I really thought it was true, that it was real. I couldn't believe that it could ever happen to me. It was so exciting to me just to be in the Olympics, let alone win a medal. That was just amazing. Still when I think back on it today, I wish I could go back and feel it all again."

As Amanda stood on the podium with that coveted gold medal around her neck, a testament to her twelve years of training, pain, and dedication, she thought of the people who had made it possible: Her training partner Jaycie, who shared the platform with her—two girls from one gym who had four years of shared experiences. Her coach, Mary Lee Tracy, who was also one of the two coaches of the Olympic team. And her family.

"Going into the 1996 Olympics, my parents probably had it harder than I did. I knew I was prepared. I knew I was ready for the competition, but my parents had to sit up there and watch me compete and just hope and pray that everything was going to work out. I couldn't have asked for a better family to support me through my journey to the Olympics."

Q: *In the year after winning the gold medal, you moved from amateur status to professional status. What was that change like?*

Amanda Borden: I really had no idea what would happen during that time. I was really not a professional athlete before the Olympics. I was planning on competing in college and that kind of thing, but after the Olympics I decided to go professional so I could go on Tour and make some money. I had no idea what to expect. I had never had an agent. I never had a lawyer. But two days after the Olympics, we are searching for an agent. It was really strange for me. Still to this day, it's weird. Gymnastics was just a recreational sport. It was just something I did after school and all of a sudden it turned into a money-maker. I wanted to make sure it didn't go to my head. I love gymnastics, and I'd never want all this agent stuff to ruin my experience. I haven't let that happen. I think that's important, because I think a lot of athletes get wrapped up in trying to make the money.

Q: *What were some perks of winning the Olympic medal, besides your professional career?*

Amanda: We got to go to the White House to meet the president. In fact, our team met the president personally right after the competition. It was really neat, because we were all kind of like, "Wow, he knows who we are." He shook our hands and congratulated us and called us by our first names. That was truly special because not many people ever get to meet the president.

Also, we got to meet a lot of other athletes. Like the men's [basketball] Dream Team. What was really exciting about that was that they were as excited to meet us as we were to meet them. They were like, "You guys are so small." And we were like, "You guys are so huge." It was kinda cool.

Touring with the team has been one of the best experiences. We are with our teammates. Nobody is under pressure. Everybody just has fun. That's what I've enjoyed the most.

Q: *What advice about sports do you give young girls you have a chance to talk to?*
Amanda: The most important thing is to enjoy what you are doing, no matter what it is. Work hard at whatever you do. Beyond that you have to have faith that no matter what happens, it is meant to be for your life. It's the best way to approach athletics. Some people are talented, some aren't. The only thing you can do is work your hardest. The rest is up to the Lord. Take the talent God has given you and use it.

Q: *Mary Lee Tracy has had a great influence on your life. What is the best thing she's taught you?*
Amanda: She helped me know how to show others how to be a Christian. When I started going to her gym, that's when I discovered what I was doing when I went to church. It was really important, because I could begin to see how my faith could tie into my life, not just as a person but also as a gymnast. She taught me that living for Christ is a daily thing rather than a church thing.

Kim Braatz-Voisard

Professional Baseball Player

ON A MISSION

VITAL STATISTICS

Born: July 13, 1969, in Santa Ana, California
Height: 5'7"
Throws: Right
Bats: Right
College: Attended Saddleback Junior College (Mission Viejo, Calif.); graduated from the University of New Mexico
Family: Married February 15, 1997, to Mark Voisard
Residence: Scottsdale, Arizona
Special Interests: Outdoor activities, reading, missions
Turned Professional: 1992

CAREER HONORS

1994: Tied for lead on Silver Bullets in assists by an outfielder
1995: Had a twelve-game hitting streak; led outfielders in assists
1996: Hit .292 with a .400 slugging percentage; had a fourteen-game hitting streak
1997: Led Silver Bullets outfielders in assists (7)

OTHER HIGHLIGHTS

1994–97: One of six four-year veterans for Silver Bullets
1996: Finished the season ranked second in eight offensive categories

WARMING UP

It's too late for Kim Braatz-Voisard, but she hopes that someday there could be women in major league baseball. "I don't think it's too farfetched," she says. "I don't think there's anyone on our team who could do it, but we started too late with baseball. I definitely think there are some young girls out there who could do it someday if they start soon enough."

FAVORITE BIBLE PASSAGE

"I have two main passages: Proverbs 3:3–6 and Joshua 1:9. The Proverbs passage is one of the first that God impressed on my heart when I began living my life for Him. I kept coming back to it and back to it. It sums up everything. I used to read just verses 3 and 4, but then my teammate Beanie Ketcham said, 'Read 5 and 6.' I had always read it, but when you meditate on it, it's amazing. When you carry it around in your pocket and you pull it out and read it throughout the day, you sort of absorb it in your spirit and you start to understand it more."

Kim Braatz-Voisard

Right-handed pitcher Pete Princey looks in for his sign from his catcher. The count is one ball, no strikes on Colorado's right-handed-hitting outfielder. The batter digs in for the next offering from Princey, waiting for a pitch the batter had seen him throw while he was warming up.

As the pitch heads toward the plate, the batter's eyes widen. It's the low fastball Princey had displayed earlier. The batter takes a mighty cut and drills the ball deep down the line in left. The left-fielder goes back to the 315-foot sign and watches helplessly as the ball sails over his head, twenty feet beyond the fence, and into baseball history.

Baseball history? A simple 335-foot home run?

Yes, indeed, it was. That home run had come off the bat of Kim Braatz, a member of the Colorado Silver Bullets, a women's barnstorming baseball team. Since the team's conception in 1994, the Silver Bullets have traveled the country to play against teams of men, usually college players or local all-star amateur teams. Braatz's poke was the first home run ever for a member of this pioneering aggregation of women professional baseball players.

Much of what the Silver Bullets had done since they first took the field in 1994 under the leadership of former major league pitcher and general manager Phil Niekro was historic. Not since the women's league whose story was told in *A League of Their Own* had women had such success with baseball. But this team was different. This was women playing against men.

As the league made its way through those first ground-break-ing years, one of the measuring sticks that was often held up to their efforts was the home run. "For the years since we were estab-lished," Kim says, "people would ask, 'Has anyone hit a home run?' Or 'Can you guys hit home runs?' That was a priority to lots of people who wanted to know if we were a legitimate baseball team."

Before Braatz connected for that home run in Cape Cod, Massachusetts, on July 21, 1996, she had told them, "You don't have to hit home runs to win ball games." But after the historic round-tripper, she realized its significance. "It was such a big step for women in baseball and our team. After I hit mine, three of my teammates hit them throughout the rest of the season. We had a total of four home runs that year."

Kim was not finished making news as a Silver Bullet, though. She collected another significant first about a year later. But first, let's look at the background of a young woman whose most signifi-cant achievement is not her strong swing but her strong faith.

The fact that Kim Braatz earns her living playing ball on a dia-mond is not surprising. The surprising part is that the diamond sport is not softball.

As a kid in Costa Mesa, California, the older daughter of Frank and Genie Braatz virtually grew up on a softball field.

"As far back as I remember, we were always at the ballfield," she says. "My mom and dad both played just about every night of the week. My dad played on a fastpitch men's league two nights a week, they played on a co-ed team, and my mom played on a women's slo-pitch team that my dad coached. We were always at the ball field."

When Kim and her sister Leah started tossing the ball around, they had a built-in coach. Kim says, "My dad coached me all the way through until I was in junior college. He always coached me when I was little. He helped coach when I was in high school. My dad spent so much time with us. We lived and breathed softball."

Not baseball, mind you. Softball.

"My dad didn't think baseball would get me anywhere. Now he says, 'I wish I would have known.' " Maybe she would have played for the Colorado Rockies instead of the Colorado Silver Bullets.

Kim did other things besides playing softball as a kid. "I played soccer and ran track. And volleyball. I loved volleyball. But everything was mostly focused on softball."

After graduating from Estancia High School in Costa Mesa, Kim took her considerable softball skills to Saddleback Junior College in Mission Viejo. And along with her, she took a problem.

She was, she feels now, an alcoholic.

She's not proud of it, but she tells about it as a way of showing the contrast between her life then and her life now. A contrast between an empty life without a Savior and a full life with Jesus Christ.

"I was a real partier," she says. "Ever since I was in high school, I was always searching for something to fill me up. I was really searching for love. When I would drink a lot, I felt like everybody loved me and everyone was my best friend. So I did it quite often.

"I was out of control. I kept searching and I kept coming up empty. When I was just out of junior college, I worked in Laguna Beach at the Ritz-Carlton Hotel where I parked cars.

"I lived with a couple of guys while I was working there. One of them was dealing drugs and getting stoned all the time. I would do it sometimes, but my problem was mostly drinking. I was just empty. Really empty."

"Then all of a sudden, a couple of my friends—the one in particular that was dealing—were on fire for Jesus. They threw everything away. They stopped everything. They went cold turkey. Only God can do that."

The deliverance of Kim's friend James was remarkable. "He had been brought up in church," Kim says of her drug-dealing, strung-out friend. "One night he had just had it. One night he came home so stoned, so drunk. He was just bawling and weeping in his room."

Later, James told Kim that on that evening, it became clear to him what he needed. He needed God. "He got down on his knees and started crying out to God. He told me that he sobered up as soon as he cried out to God—like the snap of his finger. He said God was so real to him, it was like the veil was lifted off his eyes."

Suddenly James was, as Kim says, "on fire for God."

At about the same time, Kim began to notice something that she thought was a bit odd about a guy she worked with at the Ritz-Carlton. He brought his Bible to work every day.

"He'd always have his Bible!" Kim marvels. "I started wondering why he did that. I had always believed in God, but I had always looked at God as condemning and judgmental. I didn't think I was good enough for God." It was only later that she found out that God's love for her wasn't based on how good she was, but on His own goodness. "I never thought of God as a loving God. I started wondering, 'What is in that Bible that makes him want to read it all the time?' I thought it was just a book of rules."

Despite the influence of these two friends, Braatz was not eager to jump over to their side. "I didn't want to change my life," she says.

But James was not about to give up on her. "He started talking to me, and I was just saying, 'Just leave me alone. I'm happy for you, and you needed that. You needed to get off drugs.' " But while she was saying this, she knew she was in as bad a shape as they were.

"I was watching them like a hawk. They had what I wanted. I started asking them a couple of questions here and there."

Finally, James took action. He invited Kim to go to a concert. It was something billed as a Harvest Crusade with music and a speaker named Greg Lowry at the Pacific Amphitheater in Costa Mesa.

"We went in and this place was packed," Kim says. "We sit down and this guy [Greg] starts talking and sharing. Then a man named Dennis Agazanian gets up and starts singing these songs about the Lord, but they are country songs. I was into country music at the time, and I thought, *I've never heard anything like this.*

"Next Greg Lowry gets up there again, and he starts preaching. I can't tell you exactly what he said, but he presented the gospel. It was the first time I had ever heard it. I just broke. I was bawling. I looked over at James. I said to him, 'I don't know why I'm crying.' He had the biggest smile on his face. He said, 'God just knocked on your heart, Kim.'

"The next week I went with James to Calvary Chapel in San

Clemente, and I was bawling again. I went up after the service, and I said, 'I want to be saved. I want this.' I had no idea what I was doing, but I knew I wanted it. And that's when I put my faith in Jesus Christ."

At the time, Braatz was just about to begin her first year at the University of New Mexico after spending two years at Saddleback Junior College. For the next two years, she played major college softball, which had been her goal. She was also, she says, "in the wilderness" spiritually. Unlike her friend James, who was immediately on fire for the Lord, Braatz was lukewarm. "I was in and out of church," she says. "Doing my thing. Backsliding into that old stuff."

The problem, she knows now, was that she didn't have any Christian training and accountability. "I was never around Christians. I never had fellowship. I didn't know what that was."

A successful college career on the diamond, though, did pay dividends for Braatz athletically, if not spiritually. After graduating, she took off for Italy where she had been signed to play professional softball.

While there, even though she again had no Christian fellowship, Kim began to make some spiritual progress. Again, it was because of a friend's influence that it happened. "A friend of mine had sent some tapes on the New and Old Testament, and I began to listen to them. It was so neat because the Lord was having fellowship with me while I was over there, even though there were no Christians around. Also, something provoked me to read my Bible every day."

When Braatz came back to the US, it was 1994, and the Colorado Silver Bullets were just about to begin their first season of play. Kim was given the opportunity to try out for the team, but something else had captured her heart by this time. "My heart was calling me into missions. Should I try out for the Bullets or should I go to the mission field?" she asked herself.

"I was praying, 'Lord, what do You want me to do?'"

Before tryouts were scheduled to start, Braatz received a list of the players who were going to be at a training camp to try out for the team. She knew two of the women, and she knew they weren't Christians. "It was like the Lord was saying, 'There are two reasons I want you to go.'"

Kim had to consider one more thing as she contemplated the possibilities of playing for a team that was sponsored by a brewery. As a Christian who had once struggled with alcoholism, she wondered about the rightness of playing for the Silver Bullets.

That's when some friends of hers stepped in to offer some advice. Major league pitcher John Wetteland and his wife Michelle had become friends with Kim during her time in Albuquerque at the University of New Mexico, and they were her "examples of how Christians should live."

So Kim asked Michelle what she thought. "I asked her, 'Should I be worried that they are sponsored by a beer company?'

"She said, 'Kim, every major league baseball team is backed by some alcohol or tobacco company. They just don't have their label on their jerseys. Is that to say that John or any other player shouldn't be out there because of the company?' "

Michelle then answered her own question for Kim. "She said, 'You can be a light in the darkness. Don't let that stop you from doing God's will.'

"She just made me see that they need Christians on the team. What a huge need there is!"

Braatz tried out, and she made the team.

Whether that was a blessing or not seems open to conjecture. For instance, the Bullets lost their first game 19-0 to a professional men's team—a collection of all-stars from the Northern League. Shortly thereafter, Niekro announced that the team wouldn't play male professional teams anymore.

For Braatz, the disappointments in the first season were three-fold. First, after thirteen games, she was hitting only .088 as she tried to adjust to this new game after playing softball all her life. "When you've played softball all your life, and you see the ball from the hip from such a short distance—it's just completely different to hit a baseball. That's been the biggest adjustment for us."

The second disappointment during that first year came when Kim suffered a herniated disc in her back and had to miss half the season recovering from back surgery.

Then came the worst news of all. Kim's fiancé broke up with her.

It seemed that her whole world was crashing down. "I

thought, *God, what are You doing? Isn't this what You wanted me to do, to be on this team and share with these people?*"

Despite that prayer of despair, Braatz knew she hadn't really been doing what God had wanted her to do as a member of the Silver Bullets. "I wasn't sharing with anyone," she says. "I wasn't walking as Jesus wanted me to walk."

The entire string of bad events, Braatz now thinks, was good news in disguise, for it caused her to do some needed soul-searching.

"I hit rock bottom. But I knew that things had to change. For instance, my relationship with my former fiancé wasn't God-centered. When I hit rock bottom, it was like I had scales over my eyes and they were just taken off. It was unbelievable. It was the worst pain I ever suffered, but it was the best. God showed me how He wanted me to live my life for Him. That summer is when I consider that I started living my life for the Lord."

Among those who helped direct Kim during this time of crisis were the Wettelands. "After I had that breakdown, I watched John and Michelle and how they were living their lives. I know that no one is perfect and that Jesus is our example, but I think we need to see Jesus in the flesh so we can see how the Christian life is to be lived out. That's what John and Michelle did for me."

Buoyed by her new excitement for living for Jesus, Braatz rejoined the Bullets in 1995 after rehabbing from her back surgery. She was joined in her quest to make a spiritual difference by Lee Anne "Beanie" Ketcham, a right-handed pitcher. Ketcham had been the ace of the Silver Bullets' staff in 1994, winning five games and striking out sixty-two batters in seventy-seven innings. Included among her wins was a shutout of a team from Thunder Bay, Ontario, and the team's first-ever victory in St. Paul, Minnesota. Together, Beanie and Kim had Bible studies and built each other up in their faith throughout the first years of the team's existence.

Then, in the spring of 1996, another significant person entered Kim's life. She was training in Tucson, Arizona, getting ready for her third season with the Bullets. Joining her in the training regimen was her sister Leah, at the time a catcher for the University of Arizona softball team, and Kim's friend Beanie. One day as they were on the field working out with another friend, the friend told them that a guy was coming in from Ohio to practice and needed a catcher. He asked Kim, a former catcher herself, to catch for him.

The guy from Ohio was Mark Voisard, a 6'4" pitcher for the Colorado Rockies organization. He had pitched since 1992 with Rockies' minor league teams and had been on the team's forty-man roster in the spring of 1995. Now he was coming off surgery to remove bone spurs. He was in the middle of his rehabilitation, and he needed to get in some throwing.

Kim caught him. In more than one sense. They began seeing each other soon after that first baseball-field meeting.

"He had turned his life over to Jesus Christ six months before I met him," Kim says. "His mother had passed away, and he got on his knees and accepted the Lord. It was between him and God."

As the 1996 season unfolded, Mark went back to New Haven, Connecticut, a Rockies' Double A affiliate. However, because he had not had time to rehab properly after his surgery, he was ineffective. The Rockies released him a month into the season.

As for Kim, she had her best season for the Silver Bullets. She hit .291, twelve doubles, and thirty runs batted in to go with her famous home run.

The off-season after the 1996 season was a blur of excitement for Kim. First, in December, she traveled with the baseball ministry Unlimited Potential, Inc. (UPI), to Bangkok, Thailand, on a missionary journey. Ministering at an international school, Kim and the UPI team talked about baseball and Jesus. "It was awesome," says Kim. "God poured out His Spirit, and so many kids were saved. They loved what we could do in baseball, and that gave us a platform to talk to them about Jesus."

A heart for missions still burns inside Kim, and this gave her the kind of outlet for evangelism that she had wanted since she rededicated her life to serving God in 1994.

The second big event for Kim during the off-season after the 1996 baseball campaign took place on February 15, 1997. That's when the battery-mates Kim Braatz and Mark Voisard became husband and wife.

This meant that the 1997 baseball season had a new look.

Instead of traveling solo through the fifty-plus-game schedule, she had Mark with her. The Silver Bullets hired Mark to work for the team as equipment manager.

Still, the honeymooning couple had to work to find quality time together. "People would think we were together all the time," Kim says. "But once we went to the field, it was like we weren't together. He had his job, and I had mine. Finding quality time spiritually was tough."

Yet because they were together, Mark got to experience the second historic and significant event Kim got herself mixed up in as a member of the Silver Bullets. The home run in 1996 had achieved for her a certain level of fame, but this next event, she reluctantly admits, garnered for her even more notoriety.

It was June 13, and the Bullets were in Albany, Georgia, playing the Americus Travelers, the state champions in the Georgia Recreation and Parks eighteen-and-under league. In the ninth inning, Kim came to bat with two outs, with the Bullets trailing 10-6. On the mound for Americus was Greg Dominy. On an 0-1 offering, Dominy plunked Braatz-Voisard in the back with the pitch.

Kim was headed for first base when she noticed that the pitcher was laughing at her. She did what most self-respecting baseball players do these days: She went after the pitcher. Of course, both benches cleared as everyone sought a piece of the action.

Normal baseball procedure, some would say. But this was another first—the first co-ed brawl on a baseball field.

Kim Braatz-Voisard was not happy to be the key figure in this part of history. "Unfortunately, we had more publicity over that than we did my home run," she says. "When it happened, I didn't really think at all. I just reacted."

Her biggest concern was the impact it would have on her testimony as a Christian. "I've really been torn about it spiritually. I had so much anxiety. I was so afraid that I had ruined my witness with tons of fans. I had been known for being a Christian for the past four years, and I was just so afraid of that. I kept going to Beanie and saying, 'What do I do about this? What do I say about this?'"

She continues, "I was trying to go by what Scripture says and not what man says, even our Christian fellowman. I think the bottom line was that I shouldn't have done it. I should have turned the other cheek, because I don't think that's the way Jesus would have reacted. So my intensity got the best of me."

For Mark's part, he felt that it simply demonstrated what kind of player Kim is. "Everyone else on the team said, 'I can't believe it was Kim,'" she recalls. "But he said, 'I can believe it. She's intense. She's a fiery player.'"

After all the hubbub over the event had died down, all Kim could do was trust God to make something good out of it. "I prayed so much that God would turn it around to the good."

That's pretty much what Jesus Christ has done with Kim's whole life. He took an athlete whose life was headed for destruction and turned it completely around. He has made mid-course corrections in her life that have given her a heart for witnessing about the gospel and a passion for missions.

Although many may look at Kim's team and conclude that it has a mission to open up the possibility of baseball to women, it's easy to see that Kim's mission, though it includes baseball, is much bigger.

Whether she and Mark end up in overseas work or stay home and serve God in the United States, one gets the feeling that whatever they do, their work will someday be stamped Mission Accomplished.

Q & A WITH KIM BRAATZ-VOISARD

Q: *Was your home run hit with an aluminum bat or with wood?*
Kim Braatz-Voisard: We had always used wooden bats from the beginning, and we had to work really hard to swing the wooden bats. In 1996 we switched to aluminum bats. That home run wasn't like any other ball I hit well with a wooden bat. I have a tendency to hit the ball up the middle or in the left-centerfield gap. I hardly ever hit long balls down the line. I was just trying to hit it where it was pitched instead of pulling it.

Q: *What impact do you think you are having on young girls who want to play baseball?*
Kim: First, we want people to look at us legitimately. When we first started, people would say, "Women can't play baseball. What are

you trying to prove?" Really, it was just giving women the opportunity to play baseball if they wanted to play baseball instead of softball. Why shouldn't they?

The neat thing is getting all the fan mail from the little girls congratulating us and telling us how much they look up to us. Girls tell us, "My league is trying to push me over into softball and I don't want to play softball." Now because there's a women's baseball team, she can say, "I want to play for the Silver Bullets when I grow up," instead of them saying, "I want to play for the Yankees," and people saying, "Yeah, whatever!"

Q: *What things do you do to grow spiritually?*
Kim: I think Christian music is one of my biggest encouragements. . . . I listen to a lot of praise music. Also, I'm a book fiend. Recently, I've started reading Christian fiction, like *Atonement Child* by Francine Rivers. Books make me think through the issues.

Q: *What do you and Mark have planned for the future after baseball?*
Kim: We have no idea what God has for us. My heart is in missions, but that has to be something God provokes in Mark's heart too. We took a UPI trip to Thailand in December 1997. The Lord is filling the missions need in me through those trips.

Eventually, we would like to have a ranch and a Christian camp for disabled and abused children.

THE BRAATZ-VOISARD FILE						
Year	Avg.	G	AB	H	RBI	FLD %
1994	.088	13	34	3	0	.895
1995	.221	43	145	32	12	.974
1996	.291	48	175	51	30	.930
1997	.185	42	161	30	16	.906
TOTALS	.225	146	515	116	58	.932

Jean Driscoll

Seven-Time Boston Marathon Winner
WORLD-CLASS COMMITMENT

VITAL STATISTICS

Born: November 18, 1966, in Milwaukee, Wisconsin
College: Attended the University of Wisconsin at Milwaukee; grad-
uated from University of Illinois, Champaign-Urbana
Single
Residence: Champaign, Illinois
Special Interests: Writing, performing music

CAREER HONORS

1990, 1991: University of Illinois women's wheelchair national championship
1990: Goodwill Games gold medal in 1500m (world record)
1990–96: Boston Marathon

OTHER HIGHLIGHTS

1991: Named Woman Sports Foundation Amateur Athlete of the Year
1992: Olympics Game, silver medalist in 800m (exhibition event)
1994: Established new world record in women's 10K

WARMING UP

Jean Driscoll is a national spokesperson for Ocean Spray Cranberries. In that program, she participates in the Crave to Be Your Best program, which helps sponsor scholarships for high school girls and encourages fitness and nutrition. "Whether you are five or ninety-five, whether you are 100 pounds or 300 pounds, whether you have a disability or not, fitness is important for everybody," Driscoll says.

FAVORITE BIBLE PASSAGE

"I have a different verse for each year. In 1996, it was Romans 12:12. 'Be joyful in hope, patient in affliction, faithful in prayer.'

"The fun thing about that was during my post-race interviews after the Boston Marathon, there was a reporter who asked me how I could continue to go out there year after year with all the pressure to win and everyone looking at me, and expecting me to win. He asked how I deal with that. I said, 'There's a verse in the Bible that says be joyful in hope, and all I can do is be hopeful in doing what I know I can do.'

"He said, 'Do you happen to know where that is?' I said, 'Well, yes I do.' I quoted the rest of the verse and told them where it was. In the article in the *Chicago Tribune*, the entire verse was printed. It was so fun to see that."

Jean Driscoll

If any athlete ever "owned" an event, Jean Driscoll owns the Boston Marathon. We may say Pete Sampras owned Wimbledon when he won it three times. Or Dale Jarrett owns Daytona because he has won it twice—a highly unusual feat.

Or perhaps Steffi Graff owns the US Open by merit of her many wins. Or even Michael Jordan owns the NBA Finals because of his five titles. But what they've done is no more incredible than what Jean Driscoll has done at the world's most famous 26-mile race.

Starting in 1990 with her first entry in the race and extending through 1996, Wisconsin native Driscoll captured the wheelchair division of the Boston Marathon seven straight times. And she didn't just squeak by with those victories.

In 1990, for instance, she shattered the world record for women's wheelchair marathons by six minutes. Then each year after that for the next four years, she broke the record again.

To make the essence of Driscoll's Boston Marathon success even more dramatic, think about it like this.

Remember a few years ago when Michael Jordan quit basketball to pursue baseball—playing for more than a year in the minor leagues before realizing he wasn't good enough to make it to the majors? Imagine if Michael had hung up his Air Jordans, grabbed a bat, and the following year been named American League Most

Valuable Player. Imagine that he had led the league in hitting less than a year after taking up the sport—or better yet if he had broken Joe DiMaggio's fifty-four-game winning streak or some other record.

That's a bit like what Jean Driscoll did when she first rode onto the Boston Marathon scene. A year before she first parked herself at the starting line on Patriot's Day and wheeled her way toward Heartbreak Hill, she had never won a race at the national level. In fact, she had never raced in a marathon.

Not only that, she really didn't even want to race in a marathon.

In May 1989, Driscoll won her first race, defeating a woman who had not been defeated in five years. That victory, Driscoll recalls, put her on "clouds 9, 10, 11, and 12."

When she arrived back at her home in Champaign, Illinois, and began chatting with her coach, she was presented with a new challenge. He told Jean, "You're stronger than you think you are. Why don't you try the Chicago Marathon?" Driscoll conceded, thinking it would be the only marathon she'd ever do. "I was doing it to appease him," she says.

But then something odd happened as she wheeled her way through the streets of Chicago. "I went out and qualified for Boston." Her time in Chicago was so good that she won a spot in the most prestigious marathon on the planet. With no goals but to do her best, Driscoll had achieved what many racers work years to earn.

So what would happen next? Wouldn't an eager Jean Driscoll naturally set out immediately to train for Boston?

Not exactly. "I told my coach, 'I don't want to do Boston.'"

The coach was straightforward in his response: "You can't qualify for Boston and not go and run Boston." Of course, you can. But not many people do. Wouldn't make sense.

But it made sense to Jean. "I didn't like the idea of long-distance training. Just the whole 26-mile race idea was painful to me. I had all kinds of excuses: It took too long. I was afraid of the distance. I was afraid of finding my way—of getting lost. I was afraid of not being able to finish and getting stuck out in the middle of nowhere."

Somehow, the coach won the argument, and in mid-April 1990, Jean Driscoll found herself at the starting line in Boston. "I didn't think I belonged in the race. The only reason I did the Boston Marathon was because my coach strongly suggested it. And when coaches strongly suggest things, you end up going along with it.

"Here I am on the starting line at Boston, not believing I belonged there. I had heard about the famed Heartbreak Hill, and I knew Boston was a hilly course. I had trained in Champaign, Illinois, which is as flat as a pancake. I had not trained on hills—how am I going to survive the race? I was fearful of surviving the race. But 26.2 miles later, I ended up winning and breaking the record by over six minutes—and that's after not thinking I belonged in the race."

She didn't just belong. She owned it.

And now she loves it. A race that intimidated her at the beginning has become her calling card—not just because of her success but because of the atmosphere.

"The crowd and the spectators and the media are so well-educated at Boston," Driscoll observes. "The media is becoming better educated as the years have gone by. While we are in Boston, we are seen as legitimate elite athletes competing in the most prestigious marathon in the world. Lots of times you go to a race and you feel like second-class citizens—like the race officials feel it is their good deed to let a wheelchair division in.

"But when I'm out at Boston, it's just like when I competed in the Olympics. I'm an athlete. I'm not a disabled person. I'm an athlete who needs to train six days a week, two to five hours a day in order to be competitive.

"Because of the excitement, the way they treat us, and the knowledge the people have, it's a great event."

Despite the excitement and the respect at Boston, Driscoll discovered in April 1997 that things can go wrong. In fact they went so wrong for Jean that for the first time in the '90s, she did not capture the laurel wreath.

She was done in by a hazard that only wheelchair racers have to worry about: trolley tracks.

As the 1997 race began, Driscoll knew she was in for a long morning. First, she and the other racers faced a fifteen-mile-an-hour headwind that battled them the entire race. For Driscoll, the problems of that strong, cool wind manifested themselves in some very sore hands.

"When I race, I use gloves that are like boxing gloves. I use a punching motion to make the wheels go round. I don't grab the rims, because when my wheels are going around at fifteen, twenty, twenty-five miles an hour, I could injure myself, plus I would slow the wheels down.

"When I'm racing, I punch the wheels or fan them to make them go faster. Sort of like when a kid turns his bike upside down and hits at the wheels to keep them going. You wouldn't grab them each time.

"Because of that punching motion and because of the headwind, at the halfway mark, my hands were so sore, it felt like I had slammed them in a car door. I kept opening them up to try to get blood in them. Just to get more circulation. It was such a painful last half marathon."

That wasn't the worst of it. There were still those trolley tracks to deal with.

With about four miles to go in the race, as Driscoll was flying down a hill at perhaps twenty miles an hour, her wheels hit the trolley tracks wrong, and her chair flipped over, spilling her to the ground.

Although Driscoll sustained only a couple of scratches on her elbow, her chair didn't fare as well. A tire on her specially-built racer had become disengaged from the rim. When that happens, a glue-seal is broken, and it is nearly impossible to get the tire reinflated. Vainly, Driscoll worked on her chair for several precious minutes. As she did, Louise Sauvage flew past her into first place.

As she worked unsuccessfully to put air into the tires, Jean kept looking up the hill to see if the third place woman was coming. Although she never saw her, Driscoll suddenly felt that she needed to get rolling again. "After fussing around with that tire for a long time, I decided I've got to go. I just felt that they were getting closer. I've got to go and finish the last four miles."

Flat wheel and all, she took off. "I don't remember a lot about the last four miles except that I needed to hang onto second place." Which is what she did. For the first time since 1989, someone other than Jean Driscoll won the Boston Marathon, but Driscoll's efforts showed everyone why she was a champion.

Are champions born or are they made? That question may never be answered definitively, but when Jean Driscoll was born, there was no one on earth who thought she'd be a champion. In fact, the doctors who presided over her entry in a Milwaukee hospital in 1966 told her parents that she'd never be able to walk, that she would never attend a regular school, and that she would be dependent on her mom and dad the rest of her life.

Jean was a spina bifida baby. She was born with an open spinal cord—a problem that usually bespeaks anything but a future as a world-class, elite athlete.

Jean Driscoll had several things in her favor, though. She had a loving family to encourage her, older siblings to challenge her, and a strong determination to succeed in every area where failure was predicted.

Still today, she proudly details the fallacies of those early predictions about her life.

"When I was two, I started walking," she says. "When it was time to go to school, I went to the same school my sister, Francie, had gone to. And I've been around the world without my parents."

And for good measure, she adds one more erroneous prediction. "When I was growing up, people said, 'Jeannie's going to be a secretary. That's the only sit-down job she can do.' " She doesn't relate that story to demean the occupation of secretary, but to point out that she was determined to "buck the system." She was not going to be limited by others' expectations.

"I was a determined child," she says. "I hated being babied and patronized. I felt like I had to constantly prove that I was just like my brothers and sisters. That lit a fire inside of me. I tried everything they tried. I couldn't run as fast or wasn't as skilled in some things, but I definitely tried because I wanted to fit in. I wanted to be like the other kids.

"Because of the spina bifida, I had very weak lower-body musculature. I was able to walk with below the knee braces, but my legs were not that strong."

Throughout her elementary years and through junior high, Jean was able to keep up with others. In fact, scholastically she excelled. "The only thing that could give me self-esteem was my grades. I wasn't an A student, but I was really proud when a test came back and I had higher scores. My grades were always better than the twins'. That's the only way I felt I was on a level playing field."

Jean did so well in school that her parents enrolled her in a private, college-preparatory school, seeking to take advantage of her scholastic aptitude.

With the aid of her leg braces, she began high school far ahead of what anyone could have ever predicted when she was a little girl.

But then trouble struck. Trouble in the form of something most teenagers her age wouldn't think twice about—but trouble that changed Jean's life for years.

"Two-and-a-half months into my freshman year, I had a bike accident," Jean says. She took a turn too sharply and crashed to the pavement. In the process, she dislocated her hip. It popped back in for a couple of hours, but later that night it popped back out as she walked up a flight of stairs.

It was the beginning of a long, tedious year of surgery and rehabilitation. Five times she went to the hospital for major surgery to try to repair her hip. She spent the entire year in a body cast.

"I was devastated," Jean says. "I was mad at God. But the time I was really angry was after I went through all the surgery and was finally ready to see if it had worked. They sent me home to sit up in bed and try to get flexible and get the joints and muscles flexible. As I attempted to sit up in bed, my hip dislocated again.

"I had missed my whole freshman year and half of my sophomore year for nothing. Then I was told that I was going to have to walk with crutches—and I was going to get my first wheelchair. When I heard that, I was so hurt inside. We went home from the hospital, and I would not get up and walk, and I said, 'Forget it. I've had all these surgeries, and I'm not doing anything.' But after a week, I got bored. So I got up and started walking with crutches."

Besides the crutches, Jean had to learn how to negotiate in a wheelchair. That too caused great frustration. "When I got the chair, it was like I was going through the eye of the storm. I felt like, 'God, why don't you pick on somebody else. Why are you always

picking on me? Go after Francie or Ray or Ron or Jacques [her sib-
lings] or somebody else. Get off my back. What did I do?' "

Finally, Jean was able to return to school during her sophomore year. But major adjustments needed to be made. First, she
was now "the girl in the wheelchair." Her friends had been accustomed to her being able to walk around—albeit a bit awkwardly—
in her braces. But now she could no longer do that.

As she discusses that time in her life, Jean says, "I'm going to
write a book someday and the title's going to be *Walking Is Overrat-
ed*. I wasn't comfortable with myself, and I couldn't make other
people comfortable with me."

Always before, her good grades had helped her at times like
these. But now, after missing so much school, even that seemed to
be taken away. "The home-schooling I got from the Milwaukee
public school system was inadequate," she says.

"When I went back to school, I went into my English class,
and they were talking about iambic pentameter. I was like, 'What?
What happened to commas and grammar?' I was totally lost in
that class, ended up getting a C or a D. I went into my geometry
class and was completely lost. Ended up with a D.

"All of a sudden, the only thing that had given me self-confi-
dence was gone. I ended up transferring high schools my junior
year. I went to a public school. More than anything, I wanted to
graduate with all of my classmates in 1984." Despite missing that
long period of school as a freshman and sophomore, Jean
Driscoll's determination won out, and she graduated on time.

Academic achievement may have saved the day temporarily,
but Jean was far from being home free. There was still the matter of
her rocky relationship with God.

"My family was a church-going family, but I didn't know anything about a personal relationship with Jesus Christ. I was mad at
God constantly. For the first twenty years of my life, I didn't understand why I had all these problems.

"Looking back now, it is so clear to me what God was doing,"
she says. But it was a few years before she would see that.

After high school, Jean enrolled at the University of Wisconsin, Milwaukee. The academic success she had in high school failed
her, and she flunked out of UWM after three semesters. As she

looks back on that story of failure, she knows why. "First, I was not dealing with my disability. Second, my parents were going through a divorce. They were the last couple we ever thought would get a divorce. So I was devastated by that. I just couldn't concentrate."

At this point in her life, the consideration of the earlier question, Are champions born or made? seems inconsequential. After all, Jean Driscoll was nearly twenty years old and hadn't accomplished one athletic achievement that suggested superstardom. Not only that, but this woman athlete who is now known for her Christian testimony was still on the outs with God—angry over her less-than-favorable circumstances.

What could change the direction of her life? What could point her in the way she needed to go?

As so often happens with those who are searching for purpose and meaning and goals, Jean Driscoll was directed by loving, caring people. In her case, three people each made a huge impact on her life. Three people helped her become who she is today.

The first was a nurse Jean met when she went to the hospital to have a pressure sore treated.

"I don't have much muscle to pad my skin and my bones," she explains. "The wheelchair cushion that I was sitting on in my chair wasn't working and I don't have very good feeling there anyway. I ended up in the hospital." This happened after Jean had left her first attempt at college, and she was already feeling depressed.

"I went to the hospital not knowing what I was going to do. I didn't know why I was on this earth. I had hit rock-bottom, and I was very suicidal.

"One of the nurses who took care of me was a born-again Christian. Her name was Lori O'Brien. She offered me a job in her home as a live-in mother's helper. That was when I first heard about a relationship with Christ. She explained the gospel to me, and in November 1986, I committed my life to Christ. At the time, I really didn't know what that meant."

Still, spiritual progress was being made.

The second person who provided Jean with a vital step in the direction she needed to go toward success was Dr. Hedrik, who was part of the disabled sports program at the University of Illinois at Champaign-Urbana. He had seen Jean playing wheelchair basketball and liked what he saw. He asked her to come to UICU to join their program—one of the best wheelchair programs in the nation.

Before she could do that, though, Jean wanted to prove that she could handle the rigors of college academics. So, she re-enrolled at the University of Wisconsin to see if she could succeed. This time, with new direction, she succeeded. Soon she was back in Champaign, studying and participating in college sports. It was during this time that she began to realize success in marathons.

The third person who guided Jean to the right path was Debbie Richardson. Debbie worked for UICU, and she was asked in 1992 by the women's basketball coach to put together a special half-time program to honor Jean, who by now was recognized as one of the top marathoners in the world. In fact, earlier that year, she had been voted by the Woman's Sports Federation as the Woman Athlete of the Year.

As Richardson began to put together the program, she did hours of research on Jean. She dug up so much material that she pushed for a Jean Driscoll Day—not just a half-time presentation. That day was held on February 7, 1992. As Driscoll worked with Richardson, she found something in her that she liked. "She had a joy and peace about her that I had never experienced before," Jean says.

"I knew that I wanted to get to know her and be friends with her. We stayed in touch after the event and became close friends. In April 1992, before I left for Boston, she gave me a cross necklace. She allowed me to ask questions about the Bible and God without force-feeding me.

"She invited me to go to church with her, but I didn't want to go at first. Then, out of respect, I went with her. I'm still going to that church today. In June 1992, I recommitted my life to Jesus Christ. This time I knew what it meant to trust Him."

At last, Jean Driscoll had peace. She had contentment. She had purpose in life. Soon, she was experiencing new excitement in her life—excitement that only a child of God can understand.

One of those times came soon after she trusted Christ. Jean was a member of the 1992 Olympic team, and when she went to Barcelona, she took her Bible. "The athletes' village was only a block from the Mediterranean Sea. I would work out and go to the beach and have some awesome times with God."

Besides her Bible, she soon began to find spiritual help in Christian music. "I was newly exposed to Kim Hill and Susan Ashton. I couldn't get enough of that music." Music became an even more important part of her life when she began writing songs for her own church's worship times. She would find out what the pastor was speaking about and write a song to go with it.

Today, Jean Driscoll's life is one committed to Jesus Christ. Committed to honoring Him with her racing talent, with her musical ability, with her infectious, joyous personality. She knows exactly when she learned what it means for a Christian to give it all up for God—to take faith out of the realm of the theoretical and make it really work.

It was 1994 at the Boston Marathon. She had already won four consecutive races, so she had high hopes for this one as well. But it turned out to be far more difficult than she anticipated.

"I got food poisoning two days before the marathon. The day before the marathon, I was not feeling well, and I was reading in Proverbs. I found Proverbs 16:3, which says, 'Commit to the Lord whatever you do, and your plans will succeed.'

"Right there I committed the marathon and next year's marathon and the next year's marathon and the Olympics to God. The next day I was feeling better. I was so glad I was feeling better. I had come into this Boston Marathon stronger than I had ever been before.

"The gun goes off and we start. About 10k into the race, I was feeling very weak and sick. I realized how much being sick had taken out of me. I thought about pulling out of the race, but then I remembered that I had committed it to the Lord. I couldn't pull out of the race, as sick as I was. I threw up three times during the race." To Driscoll, there could be no quitting after committing this effort to God. In her way of thinking, a commitment meant a total dedication—an all-out effort. And if that's what God wanted from her, that's what she would give.

Pushing herself beyond normal limits because she felt that's what God wanted from her, she won the race in record time. "I ended up breaking the world record and winning by twenty-three seconds.

"I was so blown away! Blown away to tears. I knew this just was not me. The next year when I went back in '95, that verse was on my mind. Now everything I do, whether it's an interview, a workout, a race, a speaking engagement, it's just a habit now—I commit it to the Lord."

Q & A WITH JEAN DRISCOLL

Q: *What has your Boston Marathon success done to your privacy?*
Jean Driscoll: When I'm in Boston, especially around marathon time, everyone knows who I am. When I'm in Champaign, I go to the post office, they know who I am. When I go to the grocery store, they know who I am. They are excited to see somebody they've heard about. It's an honor to have people admire you and recognize you, but there are times when you wish you had the anonymity. A lot of times when I go to other cities, those people don't know who I am. So I have some sense of anonymity.

Q: *How has literature made an impact on you?*
Jean: A number of years ago, I read *The Hiding Place* by Corrie ten Boom. There was a time when I wanted to read what other people were saying. I wanted to know their secrets. I wanted to be brought in on everything. I was reading the story, and there is a part of the story where Corrie and her dad are walking to the train station, and Corrie is asking some questions about what was happening around them. Her dad didn't have the heart to share with her what was happening because he knew it would be too burdensome. She kept asking him, and he said, "Corrie, can you carry my suitcase?" She said, "No, it's too heavy." He said, "Well, knowledge is like that. Sometimes it's too heavy." That broke my desire to want to know what was going on in everyone's life. Just like that. It was such a good piece of imagery.

Q: *Do you consider yourself a pioneer in women's sports or in wheelchair sports?*
Jean: Other people have said I'm a pioneer, and maybe in a small sense I am. But when I think of pioneers, I think of Sharon Hedrick, who was the first female wheelchair athlete to win an

Olympic gold medal. Nineteen-eighty-four was the first year they had a wheelchair exhibition event. Now every year since then, they've had an 800-meter event for women and a 1,500-meter event for men. Granted they are still exhibition, but she was the first to do that.

Candice Cabel is a forty-three-year-old woman who has been racing since the '70s. She took a little time off after the 1992 Olympics and Paralympics, but she's still out there. She has seen the sport grow over her twenty-year career. Candice was out there racing and winning races when training was not seen as a science and women were not that committed. So, when I think of pioneers, I think of them.

Q: *What advice do you like to give young girls whom you speak to about athletics?*
Jean: I tell them that fitness is so important. When I sign autographs, I sign them with this motto: "Dream big and work hard." That is the title to my speeches too. That's what I start out with. I tell them that they can be anything they want to be. Because there are very few people who make it into the Olympics; there are very few who get into the WNBA, or even the NBA; there are skeptical, cynical people who say, "Look, you're not going to be able to do that. There's hardly anybody who can do that." I like to turn that around and say, "Yes, there are very few, but there are people who make it. And you can be one of those people."

THE DRISCOLL FILE

Of the top ten women's wheelchair performances in the Boston Marathon through 1997, Jean Driscoll held five of those spots.

1.	1:34:22	Jean Driscoll	1994
2.	1:35:45	Louise Sauvage	1994
3.	1:34:50	Jean Driscoll	1993
4.	1:35:42	Connie Hansen	1993
5.	1:36:52	Jean Driscoll	1992
6.	1:39:31	Louise Sauvage	1993
7.	1:40:16	Connie Hansen	1992
8.	1:40:42	Jean Driscoll	1995
9.	1:42:08	Ann Cody-Morris	1992
10.	1:42:42	Jean Driscoll	1991

Mary Joe Fernandez

Tennis

QUIET STRENGTH

VITAL STATISTICS

Born: August 19, 1971, in the Dominican Republic
Height: 5'10"
Single
Residence: Miami, Florida
Special Interests: Miami area professional sports teams, golf, water
  skiing

CAREER HONORS

1982–85: First girl to win Orange Bowl in consecutive years in four junior divisions

1984: Won US National 16s and US Clay Court championships

1985: Youngest player (14) to win a US Open match

1990, 1993: Nominated for COREL WTA Sportsmanship Award

1992: Won Olympic gold medal in doubles (with Gigi Fernandez)

1992: Won Olympic bronze medal in singles

1996: Won Olympic gold medal in doubles (with Gigi Fernandez)

OTHER HIGHLIGHTS

1992, 1990: Finalist, Australian Open singles

1993: Finalist, French Open singles

1996: Won French Open doubles (with Lindsay Davenport)

1997: Won German Open

Through the 1997 season: Won seven singles titles and eighteen doubles titles on the WTA circuit

WARMING UP

Although Mary Joe Fernandez's considerable tennis talents at a very young age led to her turning pro when she was just fourteen years old, she and her family decided that it would be best for her to be a part-time pro and a full-time student until she graduated from high school. Although that move might have slowed her rise to the top echelons of the game, she is glad she did it that way. Today, she uses that fact as an inspiration factor when she addresses young athletes. "I like to tell young girls to get an education. I could have quit going to school, but I'm glad I stayed with it. It would be very difficult to go back now and get a high school diploma."

FAVORITE BIBLE PASSAGE

The Lord is my light and my salvation—whom shall I fear? The Lord is the stronghold of my life—of whom shall I be afraid? (Psalm 27:1).

When the going gets tough for Mary Joe, she recites this verse to herself. And sometimes she reminds herself of its truth when she's out on the court.

Mary Joe Fernandez

In the recent history of women's tennis, nearly all of the top players have created some kind of big noise on the tennis scene. A couple of decades ago, Billie Jean King made perhaps the biggest commotion of all when she challenged Bobby Riggs to a one-on-one, man-versus-woman showdown. Her goal was to let tennis fans know that women could compete with men. Although Riggs won the match, King's competitive showing let people know that women and men could go head-to-head without embarassment.

Others have drawn attention to themselves through less commendable efforts—such as Jennifer Capriati's problems with drugs, Mary Pierce's difficulties with her father, and Steffi Graf's tax problems. Some, like Venus Williams, call for attention with their outspokenness. Others, like Martina Hingis, make people notice them simply because they are so successful so soon.

But one player seems to hang around the Top Ten world of tennis without making much noise. Without giving tennis beat writers headline material. Without having to go on some news-magazine program and be grilled by Barbara Walters or Jane Pauley to find the real story.

Mary Joe Fernandez has quietly gone about the job of forging a highly successful career in the stressful, mostly individual sport of tennis. Sure, she has had a few minor controversies come her way. She and her former doubles partner Lindsay Davenport saw their sister-like relationship strained. She has gone on record in print as protesting exhibition matches that sometimes threaten the popularity of tour events. And the fact that she has changed coaches a few times has raised some eyebrows. But by and large, Fernandez has avoided major controversy.

Instead of controversy, her career has been marked by steadiness, an ability to battle a variety of illnesses and injuries, and a desire to grow as a believer in Jesus Christ.

A look at Fernandez's past gives a clear picture of how she can be so level headed in the on-display world of tennis.

Mary Joe was born Maria-Jose Fernandez in the Dominican Republic in the early '70s. The daughter of a Spaniard, Jose (a lawyer), and a Cuban, Sylvia (a real estate broker), Mary Joe and her family moved to the United States when she was just six months old. She has one older sister, Sylvia.

When young Sylvia developed back problems when Mary Joe was just four years old, a doctor recommended that she take up tennis as a good exercise to help strengthen her muscles. So Jose and his two little girls would head for the tennis courts. While Sylvia and her dad played as a means of therapy, Mary Joe tagged along. "My dad would bring me along," Mary Joe says, "give me a little racquet, and tell me to play by myself."

Dutifully, Mary Joe did just that, and she quickly developed some noticeably good skills. "I began to play better and better," she says. "When I was six, a coach saw me hit and told my dad that I had good hand-eye coordination."

The Fernandezes got their daughter a coach, and she began to move up the ladder as a juniors player. She was so good that one coach told her to play in as many tournaments as possible so she could learn to lose.

By the time Mary Joe was in high school, she was one of the best young players in the country. Before she could even get started with her high school career, she was ready to move into professional tennis. "My high school coach was pretty upset," Mary Joe says about her decision to forego her eligibility to go up against the best in the world.

Perhaps one of the best indications that she was ready for the big-time came in the US Open in 1985. Just a few days after her fourteenth birthday, the Miami teenager beat Sara Gomer in straight sets to become the youngest person (male or female) to capture a match at the prestigious tournament in New York.

Mary Joe turned professional in 1986. "It was kind of a natural step," she says. "I had just won the Orange Bowl 18-and-under championship, an international junior event. It was kind of like the last tournament to play."

So, the Fernandez family gathered around the kitchen table and decided that she should take that natural step. But this was not a typical tennis-parent situation. The Fernandez family wanted to maintain some semblance of normalcy for Mary Joe.

As she was turning pro, she still had another goal to accomplish while seeking tennis titles—and the family supported her in it. She wanted to graduate from her high school. Despite considerable pressure placed on her from outside the family to drop out of school and concentrate solely on tennis, she didn't do that.

She kept up with her class, maintained an A average, and graduated from the Carrolton School in 1989. Although she missed the graduation ceremony because she was at the French Open in Paris working her way into the semifinals, she got her diploma along with her classmates. "I'm glad I finished school even after I turned pro," she says. "It helped me keep life normal at that time. School was important. I had my friends who had nothing to do with tennis, and they treated me the same."

Looking back on what she did at such a young age, Fernandez seems almost surprised that she survived it. "It's a lot of pressure for a young person to be playing in such a competitive sport. There's a lot of money involved, and the press is after you all the time. You really miss your childhood, and you're expected to be grown up when you're fourteen or fifteen. When I was seventeen or eighteen, I was better equipped to take on a competitive sport."

Despite her youth, she did quite well as a part-time player during her high school years.

For one thing, she turned pro just in time to go up against her childhood tennis hero, Chris Evert, during the last few years of Evert's career. "When I was a teenager, I played against Chris a lot. I never beat her."

Yet she defeated enough people to become a successful pro. In her second year on the Tour, before she was old enough to drive a car, she was ranked 27th by the WTA folks. By the year she graduated from high school, she was ranked 12th.

Besides the rankings, on which Mary Joe has climbed to the Number 4 spot on four occasions, another significant series of tests of success on the tennis tour are the Grand Slam tournaments: the US Open, the French Open, the Australian Open, and Wimbledon.

Three times, Fernandez has reached the Finals of a Grand Slam event. Three times she has been turned back in her attempt to capture one of those coveted titles. The first two brushes with tennis's top billing came in 1990 and 1992 at the Australian Open.

In the first one, in 1990, eighteen-year-old Mary Joe reached the finals, only to go up against Steffi Graf. The German-born twenty-year-old had won seven Grand Slam titles in her previous eight tries as she faced off against Fernandez.

Mary Joe didn't make things easy for her more famous opponent, attacking her backhand and forcing her into making numerous errors. After Graf took the first set 6-3, Mary Joe led the second set 4-1 before things started falling apart. Her worst error of the day was missing an easy overhead smash that would have given her a 5-2 lead and the inside track to tie the match at one set apiece. Graf rallied to win that set 6-4 and capture the Australian Open.

Mary Joe flirted with the Australian Open title again in 1992. This time, she ran into the other top woman player of the early '90s, Monica Seles. Heading into the tournament as the seventh seed, Fernandez ran into a buzzsaw in the finals as Seles cruised 6-2, 6-3 to maintain her strong number one ranking.

Fernandez is honest about her assessment of those two battles. "The first two Grand Slams in which I played in the finals, I didn't expect to win. I was so new at it, I was just glad to be there."

Things were different by 1993. Under a new coach, Harold Solomon, Fernandez, who had been noted for her cautious baseline play, changed her tactic. Solomon convinced her to attack more.

As she did, she surprised the observers at the French Open. This quiet, unassuming lady from Florida showed she could be aggressive on the court.

The new approach began to pay huge dividends in the quarterfinals as she played Gabriela Sabatini. It looked like Fernandez's singles chances were over when Sabatini went up 6-1, 5-1. Yet the strength of the wispy, fragile-looking Fernandez carried her back. Fighting off five match points, Fernandez turned the tables on Gabby and won the second set 7-6. The third set went even longer, with Mary Joe winning 10-8 to get into the semis. The American and the Argentinian battled for three hours and thirty-five minutes in the longest Grand Slam match ever.

Buoyed by her ability to turn her new aggressive style into a victory, Fernandez then dispatched Arantxa Sanchez Vicario in straight sets, 6-2, 6-2 for the right to take on Graf in the finals.

Still determined to dictate play in the championship round, Mary Joe jumped out to a first-set 6-4 win before Graf broke loose. Steffi won the last two sets 6-2, 6-4 to take still another Grand Slam title. Although Fernandez had lost, she had shown another side to her game.

There was another notable change in Fernandez as she worked through her feelings about that French Open loss. It comes through as she thinks back to that disappointing June day. "I thought I was ready to win at the French in 1993. I was playing really well and I was healthy. But it just wasn't meant to be. When those times come, you just have to accept it and understand that God has a plan for your life, even if it doesn't mean winning the French Open."

The importance of God's plan in her life had taken on fresh meaning a few years earlier when Mary Joe made an important decision.

"I grew up going to church, and I kind of believed what my parents believed. But I really hadn't made up my mind for myself what I believed. I was talking to some of my friends, and they told me that I had to make a decision."

Those friends also recommended to Mary Joe that she do some reading. One suggested she read a book called *Power for Living*. It contained quotations from athletes who were Christians. Another friend suggested Mary Joe should read the gospel of John in the Bible.

"It really hit me that I had to make the decision for myself. I couldn't get to heaven just because of my friends or my parents. It wasn't good enough to be good or to do good things. I had to put my trust in Christ for myself."

It was a life-changing decision for Mary Joe. "Now I have a purpose and a foundation for my life. The strength I get, I know comes from God. I try to do the best I can with the abilities He has given me. Everything I do is for His glory."

Mary Joe takes her faith seriously—trying to build on it each day by praying and reading the Bible. "I try to pray every morning. Also, I like to read studies that take me to an Old Testament passage and a New Testament passage each day. I enjoy reading the Word and then doing Bible studies in the end of a study book."

The strength that Mary Joe says she gets from the Lord is of special significance to her because her career has been marked by a series of physical setbacks. They have never been anything career-threatening, but always enough to hamper her efforts to move higher in tennis echelons.

A grocery list of those injuries reveals the nagging nature of her maladies:

Shoulder tendinitis
Back spasms
Ankle sprain
Torn hamstring
Torn knee cartilage
Wrist tendenitis
Colds, viruses, pneumonia

Perhaps the most debilitating and troublesome physical problem Fernandez has faced is something that has nothing to do with playing tennis. A few years ago, she was diagnosed with endometriosis, which is a condition that allows cells from the lining of the uterus to attach themselves to other organs. It causes intense side and back pain, and the only way to get rid of the endometriosis cells is surgery. In 1993, not long after her strong showing at the French Open, Mary Joe had the surgery. Five weeks of recuperation time followed, and the recovery took many months.

It's the kind of condition that does not go away after surgery, though, so Mary Joe must still contend with it. Because of her situation, she has become a spokesperson for an awareness campaign about the condition.

Fernandez has used her fame as a top tennis player to provide assistance for others in a variety of ways. One notable effort in that regard was her efforts in 1992 to raise money for those who had been affected by Hurricane Andrew. The hurricane blew through southern Florida while Mary Joe was in New York getting ready for the US Open. For the next two days, she could not reach her family in Miami because of the interruption in communication.

Although the Fernandez home sustained only minor damage, Mary Joe wanted to help those who were more seriously hit. Later that year, Mary Joe joined three other tennis stars for a series of exhibition matches that raised money for the Andrew victims. The women raised more than a quarter of a million dollars for the hurricane victims.

Another effort Fernandez has gotten involved with more recently was the COREL WTA Tour's F.I.R.S.T. Serve Program. As a representative of the tour, Fernandez visited New York's Roosevelt High School in the Bronx in October 1997 to encourage the students to work hard and stay in school.

While there, she also revealed to the students her dream for the future. As she told them that she had stayed in high school when it would have been easier for her to drop out and concentrate on tennis, she said, "When I am finished playing tennis, I can earn my college degree and become a teacher."

Indeed, that has been her stated goal for a long time. "I love children," she says. "I'd love to be able to teach them."

As Fernandez made her way through the 1997 season, though, it did not appear that she was ready to retire and head for classes. Included in her successful 1997 season was what she would call "the biggest title of my career." In May, she traveled to Berlin and won the German Open by defeating Mary Pierce 6-4, 6-2. It was Mary Joe's seventh career singles title.

Through her steady play during the 1997 season, Fernandez showed that she was still one of the Top Ten players on the Tour. Her strong showing earned her a berth in the year-ending Chase Championships in New York, which pitted the top sixteen women on the tour.

Mary Joe Fernandez has been a professional tennis player for more than half of her life, playing before millions of people and earning millions of dollars. Yet she still strikes the observer as being unaffected and unchanged by her success. She is still very dedicated to her family, with whom she lives and whom she misses when she is on the road. And she's as enamored with her sister's two children as she is with her own impressive biography. She says, "I'd love to get married and have a family." Through it all, Fernandez continues to demonstrate quiet strength.

Even in her faith, she is quiet, observing that she "would prefer to let the testimony of the way I live let others know about my faith." Yet in her faith she is strong, depending, she says, on Philippians 4:13, "I can do everything through him who gives me strength."

Quiet and strong, Mary Joe Fernandez is one woman on the tennis tour who is worth watching and listening to.

Q & A WITH MARY JOE FERNANDEZ

Q: *You are so young, yet you've had so much success in tennis already. What would you say are your highlights in the sport?*
Mary Joe Fernandez: The two Olympics, 1992 and 1996. I won the gold in doubles and the bronze in singles in 1992 and the gold in doubles in 1996. It's a special atmosphere at the Olympics. It's different from other tournaments we play, where it's all tennis. You grow up watching the Olympics on TV, so to be there and to compete is special. Representing your country is something every athlete wants to do.

Q: *It must have been special competing in Atlanta in 1996.*
Mary Joe: Yes, it was special winning in Atlanta. But there was something special about Barcelona in 1992 and playing in front of the king and queen of Spain.

Q: *Has your career gone the way you expected it to go?*
Mary Joe: I didn't know what to expect from my career when I started. I was only thirteen or fourteen years old. There were no expectations, but I've really been blessed in my career.

Q: *Tennis is such an individual sport. It's just you and your opponent out there in front of huge crowds in person and on TV. How do you handle that pressure?*

Mary Joe: The pressure of the thousands and the millions of people goes away once I step on the court. Sure, I'm nervous before I play. There are lots of butterflies. But when the game begins, I don't think about the crowds. Just the opponent.

Jackie Gallagher-Smith

Professional Golfer

STAY TOUGH, HAVE FUN, TRUST GOD

VITAL STATISTICS

Born: December 11, 1967, in Marion, Indiana
Height: 5'5"
College: Graduated from Louisiana State University
Family: Husband, Eddie
Residence: Stuart, Florida
Special Interests: Bible study, singing, cooking, fitness
Turned Professional: 1993

CAREER HONORS

1983, 1985: Indiana State Junior champion

OTHER HIGHLIGHTS

Named All-American while at LSU in 1989
Won three tournaments on the Futures Tour
Shot a career-low 68 during the Healthsouth Inaugural in 1995
Finished twelfth on the Ladies Asian Tour in 1996

WARMING UP

Jackie Gallagher-Smith is among a group of women on the Ladies Professional Golf Association Tour who have traveled to Romania to visit with and attempt to assist children in orphanages there. Her visit there gave her a new appreciation for her faith and for her career as a golfer. "It made golf seem not so important. Golf is just something you do. It has no bearing on what life is really about."

FAVORITE BIBLE PASSAGE

Do not be anxious about anything, but in everything, by prayer and petition, with thanksgiving, present your requests to God (Philippians 4:6).

Jackie Gallagher-Smith

Jackie Gallagher-Smith is the answer to a sports trivia question: Can you name a woman who plays the same professional sport as her brothers?

Although she may not be the only woman athlete with that distinction, her situation is certainly rare. We've grown accustomed to brothers playing the same sport: The 1997 baseball playoffs spotlighted two of them in Sandy and Roberto Alomar. And finding sisters in the same sport is not that difficult. In golf, Annika and Charlotta Sorenstam. In tennis, Venus and Serena Williams.

But for a combination like the Gallagher Gang to happen is rare indeed, for it is not just Jackie and one of her brothers who share a sport—it's three siblings trying to carve out careers in professional golf.

In 1991, the entire Gallagher clan was honored by being named the recipient of the National Golf Foundation's "Jack Nicklaus Family of the Year Award." And in 1995, the Gallaghers were selected as the PGA of America's National Golf Month Family.

How does this kind of thing happen? What made this family from an Indiana town right in the heart of Hoosier hoop hysteria so different that it would turn out three professional golfers?

Perhaps it happened in large part because Jim and Jane Gallagher lived on a golf course in Marion, Indiana. And because Jim Sr. was the head PGA Professional at that course when Jim Jr., Jeff, and Jackie came along, it wasn't long until they were on the links.

"They tell me that Jim started running out on the course when he was two," Jackie says. "I figured that if I wanted any attention, I better play golf. It was a great way to grow up."

Today, Jim plays on the Professional Golf Association Tour, where he has toiled since 1983. Besides being Jackie's sister, his accomplishments have been winning five PGA tournaments: one in 1990, two in 1993, and two in 1995.

Jackie's other brother, Jeff, plays on the Nike Tour.

To make the family circle complete, Jim's wife Cissye is a former professional golfer as well, giving the Gallaghers four current or previous pros.

For her part, Jackie began getting attention from her brothers on the golf course when she began at age five. But despite the strong influence toward the little dimpled ball, she preferred spending her summers in the swimming pool. "I didn't start playing seriously until I was twelve or thirteen," says Jackie.

She also trained in gymnastics and competed on her junior high and high school teams until she was a sophomore. But as her golf game improved, her interest in gymnastics waned. By the time she was sixteen, she recalls, "I was really into golf. I didn't have much time to give to anything else."

By the time Jackie was ready to make a conscious decision that golf was the way she wanted to go, she had the advantage of having a brother who had already successfully gone through four years of college golf and was beginning his climb on the professional tour.

Jim went to qualifying school (also known as Q school) in 1983, just as Jackie was coming into her own on the course. While he was striving to make the PGA Tour that year, Jackie was showing her prowess by winning the 1983 Indiana State junior championship, an accomplishment she repeated in 1985.

Her mind was made up. With one brother already on tour, she was eager to make it a family affair. "As a high school kid, that was my goal. I wanted to play professional golf."

While Jim was battling the men's PGA Tour, Jackie was competing in a junior's event called the 1984 PGA Junior Championship. In this nationwide tournament, she tied for seventeenth place. The other girl who shot the same score was Cissye Meeks, the young woman who later married her brother.

For the next few years, as Jackie moved from high school on to Louisiana State University, her resolve was not always as strong. Perhaps it had something to do with what she observed as Jim struggled on the PGA Tour. In his first year, 1984, he ranked 148 on the money list, earning $22,249. The 1995 season went even worse as he fell to 159, with a take of just $19,061. That may not sound like bad money for a beginner, but take away the expenses for travel, hotel, and even entry fees, and there's not much left to live on. It was a tough way to earn a living.

"There were a few years in college," Jackie says, "when I wasn't sure I wanted to play pro golf. I was hearing so much stuff about how mean the players were and the tough lifestyle that I didn't want to do it."

An All-American year at LSU in 1989 may have changed her mind. "I got a lot more comfortable with what I was doing," she says. "Then I began to hear different stories about the Tour."

The next summer, in 1990, Gallagher took the plunge. After finishing her college career but not her course work for graduation, she entered the US Open as a first-time professional. That experience showed her that she was ready for the Tour. Her quest to earn a spot on the LPGA Tour would begin in 1991. First, she had a couple of other things on the agenda. To begin, in December, she completed her LSU degree. "My degree is in liberal arts, with an emphasis in business. I also took a lot of communications psychology classes," she says.

Then, about a month later, Jackie attended a wedding in Daytona, Florida, because, as Jackie says, "my friend made me go." At the wedding, besides what Jackie expected to find, she discovered a guy named Eddie Smith. Jackie and Eddie hit it off immediately, and they were married in May 1992.

With her college experience over and with her new husband at her side, Jackie continued to pursue a career on the LPGA Tour. The 1990 appearance at the US Open had whetted her appetite for the competition, and her brothers' experiences were indications that a Gallagher could indeed make a living at golf. Jim, for instance, after those first two years of subsistence-living type earnings, had by 1990 moved into the upper class of golf moneymakers. In that year, he took home almost half a million dollars.

There was no such money for Jackie as she kicked off her pro career. Between 1989 and 1993, she played in the Central Florida Challenge mini-tour, the Futures Golf Tour, and the Asian Tour, all in hopes of improving her game and winning a spot on the LPGA Tour. What she needed was an LPGA Tour player's card, a document that would open the door of opportunity for her.

Along the way, Jackie had some success, including three tournament titles on the Futures Tour.

But what she really wanted was that card. So, on October 19, 1993, she joined hundreds of other golfers at the Indigo Lakes Golf and Tennis Resort in Daytona Beach, Florida, to battle it out for the right to play in 1994. Among those at the Q school was Annika Sorenstam, a young golfer from Sweden who had already established herself as a star of the future.

Over the next four days, the women battled the Indigo Lakes course, knowing that their futures rode on every swing of the club. When the tournament was over, fifty women had earned cards. The top golfer for the weekend was Leigh Ann Mills with a 286 over the 72 holes. For her part, Sorenstam carded a 295 for the tournament to earn her playing status for 1994. And Jackie? She qualified and was just two strokes back of Sorenstam with a 297.

The fortunes of these three golfers are very much an indicator of the fickle fate of golfers. The first-place finisher, Mills, had earlier in 1993 broken onto the LPGA Tour by earning just $5,601 and placing 156th on the money list. After her first five years on the circuit, she had earned a total of $160,000, perhaps a little more than a school teacher would have made over the same time period.

Sorenstam, on the other hand, who had just a two-stroke advantage over Jackie Gallagher on that October afternoon, had raked in about $2.6 million in the same time period. Not quite a star NBA player's salary, but certainly more than enough to live on.

And then there's Gallagher-Smith. She's been playing golf since she was five. She's had great instruction from her dad and from her teacher Steve Bosdosh. She has the encouragement of her husband, and she has a strong amateur career behind her. Yet for the next four years after she qualified that day in 1993, Jackie's earnings totaled only about $80,000.

But she has learned some valuable lessons in the years since 1993, and she worked through some troublesome times to enjoy a breakthrough year in 1997—a year that may just be the impetus she needed to propel her to the kind of career she has expected for a long time.

To find the first major change in her life that affected her both for the mundane things of golf and the more important aspects of life, go back to 1993.

Less than a year after Eddie and Jackie were married, he began to attend some Bible studies. "He would come home from the studies," Jackie says. "At the time, I knew that I didn't have faith as the number one thing on my priority list. I had grown up in the church. We had gone, and I had prayed, but I didn't have a relationship with Jesus Christ."

Eventually, after continuing to ask Eddie a lot of questions, she asked him if she could go with him to the Bible study. "I had never been to a Bible study," she says. "But I went, and that was the night I accepted the Lord."

But even with her new faith, she continued to struggle to reach her LPGA goals. One of those key times came in 1995.

In order for a player to keep her LPGA card and to be eligible to play in the tournaments, she has to meet some qualifications. One of them is to finish in the Top 90 on the money list. Another is to win a tournament (some tournament wins are more important than others in determining status).

In 1995, Jackie didn't meet any of the needed requirements, which meant that for the third straight year, she had to return to Q school. In 1994, her 291 was good enough to put her back on the tour for 1995.

But at the 1995 Q school at the LPGA International Golf Course in Daytona Beach, Gallagher-Smith did not make the cut. As she approached her twenty-eighth birthday, she was back to square one as a golfer—back to the Futures Tour and back to Asia.

"That was my lowest point in golf," Jackie says. Yet to hear how she handled it and to see what she did about it is to learn an important lesson in trusting God. Sure, her heart was set on better results, but she was not defeated.

"It was a pretty big letdown, but I didn't have any doubt that I was going to get my card back. I had two other friends who were Christians, and we kind of supported each other and were there for each other. I think that helps a lot."

It also helps to know who is in charge.

She said one thing encouraged her: "Just the thought that God already has a plan for you, and even though it may not be what you want, if you follow Him sooner or later you'll find out what it was."

As Gallagher-Smith headed into the unknown of the 1996 season without a Tour card, she recalls that she "felt really confident."

Besides the strength her faith was giving her as she faced another uphill climb, she also had a couple of other elements in her favor. One was something she calls the best golf advice she has ever received, and it came from her father. It's a simple bit of advice, something that might not be expected coming from someone who is a wizened golf pro who has sent three offspring into the professional ranks: "Have fun."

That's it. Two words from Jim Gallagher Sr. "My dad has always emphasized that if you're not having fun playing golf, it's not worth doing it," Jackie says.

And then there is one more element that has aided Jackie in the past few years. It came from Deborah Graham, a sports psychologist. "I have learned to be more focused and relaxed," Jackie says. "She's taught me to play one shot at a time. I've learned not to be focused on the scores and what it's going to take to win. Plus, she doesn't just help me mentally, but she brings God into the picture—learning to trust Him. This has really helped me keep a mental balance."

So, did all this help? With her growing faith in God's control, her understanding of how to relax and have fun, and with a stronger mental game spurring her on, has there been any difference?

Jackie is convinced there has been.

"The 1996 year ended up being a great year for me," she says. "Even though I wasn't on the LPGA Tour, it was a great year mentally and spiritually."

On the Ladies Asian Tour, a short, five-week excursion through that part of the world, Gallagher-Smith finished twelfth among the golfers. And she again played the Futures Tour.

But now she played with a brand-new attitude. "For the first time, I wasn't worried about winning or being at the top of the money list." It was all part of her attempt to get her mental game in gear, something she used her Futures Tour experience to accomplish.

On October 22, she was back at Daytona Beach, joining with that host of Tour hopefuls at the 1996 Q school.

It was a new Jackie Gallagher-Smith that teed it up at the LPGA International. Confident and sure, with a game plan that she knew would work, she finished the first day of play with a 69, just two strokes off the lead held by Kristi Coats—herself a liberal arts graduate of Louisiana State University. Although both Tiger alumnae tailed off a bit in the final three rounds, they each accomplished what they set out to do—return to the Tour after not earning enough money to play in 1996. Coats settled for a 283 while Jackie posted her best Q school finish with a 285.

Jackie had done what she hadn't accomplished before. She had earned exempt status, so she wouldn't have to qualify to play each week. She could look forward to the 1997 season with renewed confidence, knowing when and where she would be playing. "It was such a relief," she says of that prized exempt card. "I felt I could play with a much more relaxed attitude."

Sports can be such a depressing endeavor. You prepare. You pray. You get ready mentally. You dive into your effort with all your being. Yet you do not know what the outcome will be. Many times, the outcome is far different from what you envisioned.

The very nature of the sport calls for that to happen. Michael Jordan doesn't make all his shots. Tiger Woods doesn't make all his putts. The Atlanta Braves don't always win. Even Martina Hingis loses an occasional tennis match.

But what happened to Jackie Gallagher-Smith as she opened up the 1997 golf season doesn't seem fair. She had paid her dues. She had learned her lessons. She had worked to improve her game.

As she stood on the first hole of the first event of the year on January 17 at the Healthsouth Inaugural at Walt Disney World's Lake Buena Vista Course in Orlando, surely Jackie looked down the fairway and saw nothing but bright skies and great possibilities.

It was a cold day for Florida, with tee-off temperatures in the thirties as the women began the tournament.

As she played that first hole, an approach shot landed in a bunker. Jackie grabbed a sand wedge and set her feet. She drew back the club, struck the ball, and began her follow-through. As she did, the club head caught the lip of the bunker. The force of the club hitting the ground sent shock waves through her arm and bruised the bones on top of her hand.

One hole into her season of hope, Jackie was injured. She finished the round with a disappointing 78 before withdrawing from the tournament.

"Oh, boy, here we go again," Gallagher-Smith said to herself. "I finally get exempt, and then I get hurt."

Trust God. Have fun. Be tough mentally. What good did all that do as Jackie now had to deal with something that none of those positive-thinking ideas could do anything about? How could she face another year of struggling in golf?

The questions that flooded her mind were answered as she thought seriously about what God was doing in her life through the injury. "God builds your character through trouble times," she concluded. "He wants you to draw closer to Him when you have difficulties. Sometimes He puts you in a situation because He wants your total love and commitment."

Confident that a good God had a good reason for her difficulty, Jackie began to make the most of it. She continued to depend on the fellowship and encouragement of friends on the LPGA Tour who participate in small-group Bible studies. She knew that those women cared for her for who she was, not for what golf score she shot.

Determined not to let the 1997 season defeat her, Gallagher-Smith worked to rehabilitate her wrist and get back on the Tour. Slowly, she began to assert herself. In early March, she finished forty-second in the Welch's/Circle K Championship, earning her first LPGA money since 1995: $2,063. The next week, she finished seventy-first at the Standard Register Ping. Obviously, Eddie and Jackie were not out looking for a new Lexus on those winnings, but after such an inauspicious start in Florida, she was just happy to be making progress.

In April, Jackie finished in the money at the Susan G. Komen International. Her next paycheck came in early May at the Sara Lee Classic, her favorite tournament. "It's in Nashville and it's a lot of fun. They have a lot of entertainment, including Amy Grant."

She made it two in a row, finishing sixty-seventh at the McDonald's LPGA Championship in Delaware. By now, Jackie was hovering around the 150 mark on the money list; it was May and she had earned about $6,000. Yet she plugged away, still positive. Still confident. Still sure that God had her there for a reason.

Slowly, she began to creep up the money list. On July 14, she was 139th. By July 21, she was up to 131.

Golfers have their sights set on certain milestones. For Jackie, the goal was 90. At ninetieth on the list, a golfer earns exempt status for the next season. It means no Q school, and it is a guarantee of another year on the Tour.

A thirtieth-place finish at the Du Maurier Classic in August moved Jackie up to 115. When she fired a 206 to finish seventeenth at the State Farm Rail Classic on September 1, Jackie stood at number 107.

In late September, her 275 at the Fieldcrest Cannon Classic gave her a fifteenth-place finish and helped her climb to 96th place—for the first time, she was in striking distance of 90.

Then, on October 5, Gallagher-Smith was in contention for the CoreStates Betsy King Classic. When she ended with an eleventh-place finish, she had moved to 89th spot on the list and had moved her earnings for the year to more than $68,000. She had earned exempt status for 1998. There was no need for going to Q school.

It had all paid off. She had overcome so much to get there. The missed cards. The Futures Tours. The doubts. The injury.

But as the 1997 season wound down, Jackie Gallagher-Smith knew that she had done the right thing. She had stayed strong in her faith, and she had stayed tough in spite of the problems.

She had put together the kind of year a family could be proud of—even a family with not one, not two, but three professional golfers.

Q & A WITH JACKIE GALLAGHER-SMITH

Q: *What is one thing you'd like to change about the way things are in professional golf?*

Jackie Gallagher-Smith: There's no other way to do it, but I don't like the money lists and being compared to other people in that way. That's really hard. I think it would be neat if there was some other way of doing it without ranking people that way. It becomes a definition of your character and ability, and sometimes it's not really true. Everything is based on money. That part of it is bad.

Q: *What's something that golf fans do that bothers you?*

Jackie: This is something that happens when I go see my brothers play. They don't know who I am, and they'll say things like, "Man, Gallagher, how could you do that? I could make that shot." They don't know what they are saying.

Q: *What do you like to do to stay strong spiritually?*

Jackie: I like to do Bible studies with guides. For instance, one I read recently was *God's Guidance* by Elizabeth Elliot. I read the chapters and then enjoy doing the study guide that goes with it. I think anything that makes the Bible applicable.

Q: *While on tour, what helps you spiritually?*

Jackie: We have a Bible study with Cris Stevens, who leads the study on the Tour. That has definitely gotten me through a lot of hard times, especially the first few years on tour. It's a great way to get away from golf, and focus on what's important. I sometimes meet with other golfers like Betsy King and Suzanne Strudwick. I lean on Cris for comfort and advice. I know I can always go to her.

THE GALLAGHER-SMITH FILE

Year	Number of events	Best finish	Money	Rank	Scoring average
1994	18	T15	$10,107	155	75.05
1995	19	T9	9,125	163	75.41
1997	25	11	$68,449	89	72.75

Kathy Guadagnino

Pro Golfer; 1985 US Open Champ
GOLF MOM

VITAL STATISTICS

Born: March 20, 1961, in Albany, New York
Height: 5'9"
College: Attended Tulsa University; graduated from South Florida
  Bible College
Family: Husband, Joe; two daughters, Nikki and Megan; one son,
  Joseph
Residence: Boca Raton, Florida
Special Interests: Crafts, Precious Moments, church activities
Turned Professional: 1983

CAREER HONORS

1985: US Women's Open
1988: Konica San Jose Classic

OTHER HIGHLIGHTS

Won National PGA Junior championship, 1979
Two-time college All-American at Tulsa
Member of 1982 US Curtis Cup team
Earned more than $130,000 in 1985 on the LPGA Tour

WARMING UP

One of Kathy Guadagnino's favorite golf courses is called Devil's Elbow at Moss Creek. She played the course as an amateur and a couple of times as a pro. "I played in it the first year of college. I went out and played pretty well. I had recently become a Christian. When I went into the pro shop, I noticed they had some buttons that said, 'Beat the Devil.' I thought that was so appropriate. And I picked up a couple of them because as a new believer, I knew that was what I had just done."

FAVORITE BIBLE PASSAGE

But seek first his kingdom and his righteousness, and all these things will be given to you as well (Matthew 6:33).

"I've always kept that in my heart. It reminds me that I need to always keep God my priority, seek Him first, and He'll take care of the rest. With that in mind, things seem to fall into place."

Kathy Guadagnino

Kathy Guadagnino appears to be a typical mom. She has a devoted husband named Joe. She has three young children who need Mom around. She struggles to find time to fit everything into an increasingly busy, complicated schedule. Just like any other mom you might see hauling the brood around in the minivan.

However, when you begin to get into Kathy's life, you realize that there's a lot more to this Florida mother than appears on the surface.

For starters, she has a master's degree in biblical studies. And her husband has an earned doctorate in Christian counseling. And she's a pastor's wife as she and Joe attempt to plant a new church in their community.

That would surely be enough to let you know a bit about Kathy Guadagnino—enough to help you see how busy this "typical mom" is.

But wait! There's one more little thing.

Kathy Guadagnino is also a professional golfer. For proof of that fact, just look at the record books. Guadagnino has to her credit one of the most prestigious victories in women's golf.

She won the 1985 US Women's Open.

Well, actually Kathy Guadagnino didn't win the 1985 US Open, Kathy Baker did. Back then, she was twenty-four years old, single, and in her third year on the LPGA Tour.

Baker's win at the Baltusrol Golf Club in Springfield, New Jersey, on that July Sunday made her one of only thirteen golfers to make the US Open their first win on the Tour. And it helped her make a long-range decision about her career.

Although she had begun to make a good living at golf, Baker was not sure she was going to stick with it. She had made $54,418 in 1984, while playing a full slate of tournaments. "I had come out on tour, but I wasn't sure how long I wanted to stay out. I knew the Lord had a purpose for my being out there.

"I had been at the University of Tulsa for four years, but I hadn't graduated. I was about a semester short. I had qualified in August 1983 to play on the LPGA Tour. That was my plan. But if I hadn't made it, I would have gone back and finished school."

The victory at Baltusrol, then, helped her decide to stay out on tour.

Heading into that tournament, Baker had an impressive résumé from her days at Tulsa. She was a two-time All-American at Tulsa, a member of the 1982 US Curtis Cup team, and the individual winner of the 1982 NCAA golf title. In both 1981 and 1982, she was the low amateur at the US Open.

Young Kathy Baker's rise to the top of golf had happened quite quickly. She didn't begin playing until she was thirteen years old. While living just outside of Charlotte, North Carolina, with her father (her parents were divorced), Kathy had gone on a spring break vacation, during which she and her dad went out to hit some golf balls. Her dad noticed that she had some natural skills in golf, so he encouraged her to take up the game. Soon after that, she entered her first junior event and finished second.

Kathy played on the boys' team at her high school because there was no girls' team. As she continued to improve, her dad decided that she might be good enough to earn a college scholarship. So, when he heard that there was a tournament in Gainesville, Florida, with several colleges represented, he and Kathy went— hoping to meet some of the coaches.

What he didn't know was that the Association of Intercollegiate Athletics for Women (AIAW), the governing body for women's sports in those days, had some stringent rules against that kind of activity. Coaches weren't supposed to talk with recruits unless the student was visiting the school.

When Kathy and her dad approached Dale McNamara, the Tulsa coach, she said to Kathy, "Well, Kath, I can't tell you anything about our school, about our program. Nothing. So, how's your love life?"

Despite that wrinkle in the recruitment process, Kathy liked what she saw of Coach McNamara. "We just seemed to hit it off from the beginning." Later, Kathy took her legal recruiting trip to Tulsa—and included stops at Furman and Southern Methodist University.

While she was in Tulsa, the worst possible thing for a golf recruit happened. It snowed. There was about six inches of snow on the ground when she arrived. Later, Coach McNamara told Kathy that she said to herself, "Oh, great. She'll never want to come with all this snow on the ground."

Baker, though, was not deterred. "There was something about Tulsa that told me it was where I needed to be."

During Kathy's freshman year at the school, she found out why.

It all began in the fall when another student came to Kathy's dorm room to take a survey. "She just started asking some questions," Kathy recalls. "The first thing she asked was, 'Are you a Christian?'

"I was like, 'Well, I think my dad is Episcopal and my mom's Presbyterian, so that makes me Protestant.'

"She was like, 'No, no, no, that's not what I mean.'"

Kathy kept going, trying to answer the question. "I said, 'I'm an American.' I just didn't know what she was asking me.'

"Finally, I looked at her and said, 'Well, what are you?'

"She answered, 'I'm not any denomination, but I have a personal relationship with Jesus Christ.'

"I remember looking at her and saying, 'You have a what? What do you do with Him?' I didn't know what she was talking about. I had never heard that before. We weren't churchgoers or anything like that. So I just had never heard of anything of that sort.

"We talked for about two hours. She gave me a Bible and wrote her name in the back. And she said, 'If you ever have any questions, just give me a call.' She kept coming through a couple of times, and I didn't want to talk to her."

At about the same time, another Tulsa student began to talk to her about Jesus Christ.

"One of the quarterbacks on our football team was president of the Fellowship of Christian Athletes chapter on campus. His name was Skip, and he was in a couple of my classes, and we started studying together. Through his input—some of the questions he asked me and some of the Scriptures he explained to me—I began to understand about trusting Jesus Christ. One day, he said, 'Kathy, the reason you're having such a struggle is that the devil is aware that you are close to making a decision for Christ. That's why you feel that conflict within you.'

"Then Skip said, 'Kathy, let me ask you this. If you were to die today, do you know for sure that you would go to heaven?'

"I remember thinking about that. I hadn't been a bad person or killed anybody. I told him that, and he said, 'The Bible says it is by grace you are saved through faith—it is not of yourself. Not according to works, lest anyone should boast.'

"Then Skip said, 'Hey, I've got to go.' With that, he took off and I was left to think about what he had told me.

"Those statements really bothered me because according to what Skip said, I wasn't there. That really bothered me. I remember I lost sleep over that for the next week. Finally, I decided that if I'm going to become a Christian I might as well find out what I'd be missing. I had my deviant week. If anything, the stuff I did that week scared me into my decision.

"I ended up sitting in my dorm room one night, struggling with doing what I knew I should do. I would start to pray, and then I would say, 'Come on, Kath! You're just talking to air. Roll over. This is ridiculous.'

"Finally, I got to the point where I sat on the edge of my bed and said, 'All right, Jesus, I believe that You died for me. I know I'm a sinner and I ask You to come into my heart and forgive me of my sins.' I did that without anyone else around.

"I sat on my bed and waited, but nothing happened. I was extremely put out. I had made this great declaration, and God didn't bother to show up to welcome me in. I went to sleep.

"The next week, everything possible that could go wrong did.

I remember thinking, 'OK, God, this is great. I'm going to tell everyone to become a Christian so this kind of thing will happen to them.'

"However, there was a definite joy I had throughout that week. The way I like to describe it is like I was living in a black-and-white world, and someone came in and painted colors for me. I remember walking out the dorm one day and getting blown away by the awesomeness of a leaf. God just really opened my eyes to creation.

"What was really neat was that when I was packing up my stuff to go home for the summer, I found the little New Testament the girl doing the survey had given me. Her name—Debbie—was on the back. I thought, *I need to give her a call, because she doesn't know that I've accepted the Lord.*

"I called her up . . . and I said, 'I don't know if you remember me, but my name is Kathy Baker. You came into my dorm room one day and you talked to me.'

"She said, 'Oh, yeah, Kathy.'

"I said, 'I just wanted to let you know that I have accepted the Lord, and I wanted to thank you because you were a big part in that. I really appreciate what you did.'

"She started crying on the phone and she said, 'Oh, Kath, I can't tell you what this means to me. I've been really having a hard time thinking that God hasn't been using me and feeling like I haven't been doing anything for Him.'

"God really used me to encourage her. That was really neat. It helped me see that God's timing is perfect."

Several years later, as Kathy Baker took on the LPGA world at the 1985 US Open, she again learned lessons in God's timing. She was in the middle of deciding whether God's purpose for her included the pro tour. As she headed into the US Open, she was beginning to get some signals that this would be a special event for her.

The first came a couple of weeks before the tournament as she was visiting her dad. "I was doing something in my room and I had a tape on of Morris Chapman. Sometimes you're listening to music and something that is said really hits home. One of his songs was 'God Is About to Do His Greatest Work in You.'

"For some reason, it really hit home in my heart. I went,

Hmm, that's interesting." She didn't know it at the time, but her greatest golfing work was about to happen. Perhaps not the idea Morris Chapman had in mind when he wrote his song about God's spiritual blessings, but a great event nonetheless.

"Two weeks later, going into the week of the Open, things were kind of crazy. I had a four-hour layover in Dulles Airport because of bad weather. Everything was happening, and none of it was good.

"When I finally got to New Jersey, I talked to my caddie, Scottie Thompson, who is also a Christian. I said, 'You know, something good is going to happen, because it's been really crazy so far.' Lots of times when I sense I'm getting a lot of opposition, I feel like something good is around the corner. I didn't realize how good at the time." She was about to embark on the best weekend of golf in her life—an event that Kathy feels is one of those special blessings God gives His children.

On Thursday, Baker shot a 70 to finish the day one shot behind the leader. On Friday, a 72 put her two strokes back.

But Saturday was the day. It was a day that she wishes she could have captured and bottled for later use. She shot a 72 to race into the lead over fellow University of Tulsa graduate Nancy Lopez.

"On Saturday," Kathy says, "the thing I did that I'm still trying to capture now is that I had such tunnel vision. They talk about getting into the zone. That's all I can say, because I didn't really notice any distractions or anything. I made four birdies on the backside that Saturday, so it wasn't like I was in the hunt, but those four birdies put me right in the front."

Now she was on the verge of her biggest win ever. "On that Saturday night, I remember feeling a sense of awe and just sensing that God definitely had His plan. I remember praying, 'Oh, Lord, don't let me mess this up.'

"I just wanted Him to be glorified, however He wanted to do it. It was kind of scary in itself because I felt like there were more things at work than just me going out and playing."

Lopez was seemingly poised for a takeover, though. In her previous six tournaments, she had won three, finished second twice, and gotten third once. Surely her experience and savvy would lead her to the victory.

On Baker's side was some wise golf advice someone had given

her: Think of one shot at a time. "That's the one thing that kept going through my mind. Concentrate on one shot at a time. Don't worry about scores. Don't worry about your last shot. Just do one shot at a time.

"I remember at the Open, coming into the last hole. I had a little putt to finish. My caddie started talking about something totally unrelated to what was going on at the time, and I turned to him and said, 'Scottie, I've still got work to do. Let me finish this, and we'll talk about it.' "

And finish she did! While Baker was shooting a 72, Nancy Lopez was struggling through a round of 77. For the tournament, Baker shot an 8-under-par 280, the second best score in US Open history.

Suddenly everything changed for Kathy. It started to set in the next day as she participated in an event that had been scheduled before she had won the biggest tournament of her life. "I remember sitting there the next day when I had a few minutes to myself, and I said, 'You know, Lord, this is really great. I've just won the US Open! But what have You just done to my life?' "

For one thing, she was no longer an unknown commodity. "People were recognizing me in the airport. All of a sudden from basically nobody knowing who you are, your privacy seems to be gone and people start recognizing you. That took some getting used to."

There was the TV coverage: "I was on David Hartman's morning program. I had to go to downtown Boston at five in the morning to do that."

There was the print media: She was the subject of a *Sports Illustrated* article called "Opening in High Style," which emphasized the fact that Kathy had won a beauty contest and that some people mistook her for Jan Stephenson.

"The requests for interviews [were] hard. For the next several weeks, whenever I came into a new town, I had to do a lot of interviews. I had to learn to pace myself.

"I finished out the year pretty well. I finished thirteenth on the money list. I had a lot of opportunities as a result. It was an exciting time."

For the next couple of years, Kathy continued to play the

LPGA Tour without a victory. In the meantime, in addition to earn-ing a decent living playing golf, she also completed her bachelor's degree and began working on a master's degree at South Florida Bible College and Theological Seminary.

At the same time, she began attending Christian Love Fellow-ship, a church in Deerfield Beach, Florida. While there, she noticed that the pastor had three children. Then one day a new guy showed up at church. Someone pointed him out to Kathy and said, "That's the pastor's other son."

Kathy responded, "What other son? I didn't know he had another one."

He did. Guy named Joe.

"I remember looking at him and thinking, *Boy, that's trouble.* He had it written all over him."

Soon, though, she changed her tune and decided that Joe Guadagnino was somebody she would enjoy being around. As she got to know him, she enjoyed his company and was impressed with his love for Jesus Christ. But there was one problem.

"I had never dated anyone shorter than me, which Joe is." One day she decided to call the whole thing off.

"The next day, I was reading in the Bible. I read about Samuel when he was going to the house of Jesse to anoint the next king. He didn't know which son it was going to be. He sees Eliab, and he thinks this is the one he has chosen. The Lord said to Samuel, 'Do not look at his appearance or his height.'

"The word *height* just jumped right out at me. It says, 'For I've rejected him, for I don't look at the things man looks at. I look at the heart.'

"That was one thing I knew about Joe. His heart was sold out to God. It was just so funny. Talk about an immediate answer! I said 'too short,' and the next day I read this passage.

"We were engaged shortly after that, and we were married on June 20, 1987."

The next year, Kathy Guadagnino captured her second LPGA victory when she won the Konica San Jose Classic. That victory pushed her to her second-best year on the money list as she won $71,912 to finish forty-third on the list. That would be the last win for her on tour.

Now there are other priorities on Kathy's list.

As the wife of a pastor, as a mother of three, and as a professional golfer, she sometimes feels that she can't give any of her responsibilities top billing. "Sometimes I feel like I'm doing everything half of what I should. I'm a part-time mom, part-time golfer, part-time pastor's wife. It's hard to juggle all those.

"It's been hard because I'm playing part-time. Since my last victory, I've had three kids."

Although it's difficult to balance her priorities, she says, "I still have some contractual obligations on tour. I want to play those out, and it's good for us as far as income, because we don't have a lot of income starting a new church.

"This all gives us an opportunity to be dependent on God. In the financial area, I've never been hurting because I've had success. In the past few years, because I haven't played all that well, I remember realizing, 'Lord, I believe You'll supply all my needs according to Your riches in glory.'"

But it hasn't been easy for her as a mother or as a golfer. "I'm balancing so many different things at this point." She has trouble finding time to practice as much as she needs to. "I go out there, and my game is not as sharp as it could be. That part is hard to handle. Shots that I used to be able to do in my sleep, I struggle over. When you see your game going backward, that's hard to deal with."

By playing just a handful of tournaments a year, Kathy has cut way back on her golf earnings. For instance, the 1997 season saw her win just a little more than $14,000. Yet she presses on.

"We're in a position in which we're just having to believe God. Once you let go of the reins, it's very comforting, knowing that He is taking care of you—to see His provisions as they come strengthens your faith."

As Kathy Guadagnino ventures out for her golf outings, one of the big decisions she has to make is whether or not to take the family. For one trip to a New Jersey course that was close to Atlantic City, she and Joe decided to take the family.

"Even if I don't make the cut, we can turn it into a vacation," she says, describing the thought processes of a mom-on-tour. Then she adds, "We have to think about the baby, Joseph. He's a homebody. He'd rather be in his own crib at home."

Yes, just like any other mom, Kathy Guadagnino is more concerned about the welfare of her children than she is about which golf course she plays best.

Q: *Did you ever, in your wildest dreams, think you could win the US Open?*
Kathy Guadagnino: Two years prior to it, I was playing a practice round out at Cedar Ridge, in Tulsa, for the Open that they had there a couple of years before the one I won. We were walking up 18 and I remember looking at my playing partner and saying, "You know, I'm going to win the US Open."

It was one of those things. It was out of my mouth before I even thought it. I kind of shocked her. It kind of caught her off guard. She said, "Well, what was that, a faith statement or what?" I said, "I'm not really sure what that was."

Q: *What is your biggest challenge now in golf?*
Kathy: The biggest challenge is the mental aspect of the game now. That's one thing I used to be pretty strong in. When you're younger, you don't have as many things to think about. You just go out and think about golf. I don't have that luxury anymore. It's even that much more of a mental discipline for me to play.

Q: *What literature has been really helping you recently?*
Kathy: I've been reading a lot of stuff by John Maxwell, who writes on leadership. It is helping me become more of a people person. In college, I majored in psychology because I felt I would be dealing with people the rest of my life, so I might as well find out what makes them tick. Since I've been married, I had a chance to help my husband as he pursued a Ph.D. in Christian counseling. We really found out a lot about each other. I've found that Maxwell identifies different personality types, and they help put things in perspective. The Lord is trying to unify the body of Christ, and it helps if we have a better understanding of each other.

THE GUADAGNINO FILE

LPGA Record

Year	Number of tourneys	Best finish	Money	Rank	Average strokes
1983	6	T34	$1,456	153	75.50
1984	26	2	$54,418	35	73.53
1985	26	1	$132,643	13	72.77
1986	21	T8	$47,069	54	73.26
1987	21	T2	$43,847	55	73.42
1988	21	1	$71,912	43	73.46
1989	19	T8	$30,110	86	73.96
1990*	11	T29	$12,653	135	74.78
1991	18	T18	$18,902	127	74.24
1992**	16	T21	$16,631	137	74.23
1993	18	T8	$58,661	80	72.69
1994	21	T23	$26,318	121	73.67
1995	16	T26	$16,458	144	74.97
1996***	12	T59	$2,360	191	76.11
1997	14	69	$14,319	159	75.24

*First child, Nikki, was born in 1990
**Second child, Megan, was born in 1992
***Third child, Joseph, was born in 1996

Nancy Lieberman-Cline

WNBA; Member Basketball Hall of Fame
A SENSE OF HISTORY

Born: July 1, 1958, in Brooklyn, New York
Height: 5'10"
College: Old Dominion University
Family: Husband, Tim Cline; son, TJ (Timothy Joseph)
Residence: Dallas, Texas
Special Interests: Tim and TJ; sports broadcasting; charities such as
    Special Olympics, Juvenile Diabetes, Girl Scouts

CAREER HONORS

1975: Gold medalist, Pan Am Games
1976: Silver medalist, US Olympic team
1978–80: All-American at Old Dominion
1979, 1980: Wade Trophy Winner
1980: Named to Olympic team; US boycotted Games in Moscow
1979, 1980: Led Old Dominion to national championship
1984: WABA All-Star Game MVP
1986: Became first woman to play for a men's pro league, United States Basketball League's Springfield Fame
1996: Named to the Naismith Memorial Basketball Hall of Fame

OTHER HIGHLIGHTS

At 18 was the youngest basketball player in Olympic history to win a medal
Only athlete to receive the Wade Trophy twice
Has played in four professional basketball leagues
Was a member of the Washington Generals, the companion team to the Harlem Globetrotters (1987 & 1988)
Played with Athletes in Action in 1996 and averaged 15.7 points per game
Named coach of the WNBA Detroit Shock (1998)

WARMING UP

Nancy Lieberman-Cline has seen the whole atmosphere of women's basketball change. One way it has become different is in the relationships she is noticing. "It's a glorious time right now for girls and their dads. Before, moms were always dragging their kids over to practice. Now you're seeing that real relationship between daddies and their little daughters. You're seeing them in the schoolyards, you're seeing them in the park. You're seeing dads taking their girls to practice. Like they would if they had a little boy.

"For me, it's a little different. I have a little boy. It is the coolest thing for him to be sitting in the stands while I'm playing and be saying, 'Mommy! Mommy! That's my mom!' And he's wearing a replica of my uniform. It just brings tears to my eyes."

I can do everything through him who gives me strength (Philippians 4:13).

"Every day is a struggle to make sure you put things in God's hands and understand you're not running the show. Whenever it comes down to some decision, I know I can trust God, and He'll work things out."

Nancy Lieberman-Cline

What was Nancy Lieberman-Cline thinking? Here she was, arguably the best women's basketball player ever. A two-time Olympian. A member of the Basketball Hall of Fame. Happily married and the mother of a cherished little boy. A successful businesswoman who had her own basketball camps and a respected career as a basketball analyst for ESPN.

Here she was, thirty-eight years old. Older than Magic Johnson. Yet here she was, willing to work herself back into playing shape on the basketball floor for a shot at her fourth professional basketball league.

What was she thinking?

In a sense, she was thinking what she had been thinking ever since she was a Jewish girl growing up in Queens, New York. Back when she would grab a basketball and head for the playgrounds to escape the turmoil of a broken home and a mother with whom she was constantly fighting.

She was thinking about her love for basketball.

"Throughout my whole life," says the energetic, dynamic woman who has retained just a delicious hint of her New York accent, "nothing made me happier than picking up a basketball and playing. When my parents were divorcing, when I was just miserable, when I felt like I had nothing else—way, way, way back then—being on that court put a smile on my face. Being on the court gave me confidence. It gave me self-esteem. Playing ball had been everything to me, especially in my formative years, especially before I knew anything about God. It was what I depended on. I have such a passion to play."

In a sense, Nancy Lieberman was to women's hoops what Pete Maravich was to men's. Maravich, who claimed to be a basketball android, made the basketball court his private haven. He, like Nancy, grew up in the era before basketball was as hot as it is—yet they both had a love and a drive that propelled them and the game to new heights. To both, there was no greater happiness than being on the hardwood—especially because being off the court meant facing life's struggles, of which both had many.

So the first thing Nancy was thinking was about the love she had for the game.

Before the new leagues (the ABL and the WNBA) began to take shape in 1996, Nancy wondered if her time had come and gone too soon. "I used to go through this line of thinking: Maybe this is not meant to be. Maybe this is not in God's plan. It's in my plan, but not in His. Maybe a valid pro league is not going to happen in my lifetime.

"I really struggled with that. I wanted to play so bad, but there was nothing for me. And I started seeing this league and this situation emerge, and it was really strange, but in my heart I knew it was the right thing to do."

The second thing Nancy Lieberman-Cline was thinking was that she could fulfill her own dream of playing in a league that had wide acceptance and viability.

But there was something else. Something a woman who had been a nationally known basketball player for more than twenty years understood far better than any of the young people who became her teammates.

"I was willing to put my reputation on the line. My reputation was set. I was at peace with my contribution to the game. But I thought I could be inspirational not only to me, by doing something I loved, but to the young players. If there was a young girl—if there was a Sheryl Swoopes or a Lisa Leslie or Rhonda Blades and they really loved this game—they could look at me and say, 'Oh my goodness. I can't believe she's thirty-eight or thirty-nine and she's doing this stuff. Maybe I can do that when I'm her age.'

"Everybody needs a Robert Parish or a Warren Moon out there who can say, 'Hey, if you really like this, you can do it.' I knew I wasn't going to be a superstar, I knew I was going to be a role player, but I was fine with it. I wanted to play."

It was also a sense of history that Nancy was thinking about. A tie between the stars of the past and the stars of tomorrow. She explains that idea by talking about a practice scene that she enjoyed as a member of the WNBA Phoenix Mercury during the 1997 season.

"You should see me everyday in practice running suicides with a smile on my face. The kids on the team are looking at me and saying, 'What is wrong with you?'

"I'd say, 'I waited twenty years to do this. I waited twenty years to be your teammate.' I could be such a good voice in the locker room. I could share the history of the game. How do these girls know what happened in the '70s or '80s? They have no clue. They only know that they are twenty-two years old and they're making money and they're being given things, and this is the way it's supposed to be. If we don't share the history, then shame on me."

It was a sense of history that carried Lieberman-Cline into the Women's National Basketball Association. And it was the advice of a famous friend who helped her solidify her decision to play.

During late summer in 1996, Lieberman-Cline committed herself to playing on the Athletes in Action (AIA) team that traveled around the country and played against college teams while witnessing about Jesus Christ.

But then, ten days before she was scheduled to leave for the AIA tour, Nancy got a call from the American Basketball League. The ABL had snared some of the top women's players from the college ranks and from the Olympic team, and league officials recognized the value of history when they asked Lieberman-Cline to sign with them.

The ABL offered Nancy $125,000 to play in 1996 and $150,000 to play in 1997. "When somebody does that, you want to look at it," Nancy understates. "You don't want to look stupid. So, I talked it over with my husband."

And Kevin Costner. "Kevin is a friend, and I was talking it over with him," Nancy says. "I explained the situation to him, and I thought, *He's been in this kind of situation before; I'll get his opinion.*

He asked her a couple of questions: "Are you playing for the money?"

"No," Nancy answered.

"Are you playing to be a part of history because you love what you do?" came Costner's second question.

"Yes," was Lieberman-Cline's response.

He said, "Do you think the ABL will be here in twenty years?"

"I don't know if it will," replied Nancy.

"Do you think the WNBA will be here in twenty years?"

"I think so," said Nancy.

"You just made your decision. You want to be a part of history."

"He was right," Lieberman-Cline says. "He simplified it for me. Plus, I had already made my commitment to AIA, and I really didn't want to break that. I thought it was a matter of integrity. So many athletes commit to something and somebody pays them more, and they go to the next thing. And I just didn't want to fall into that category."

So, on June 22, 1997, just shy of her thirty-ninth birthday, Nancy Lieberman-Cline suited up for the Phoenix Mercury in what proved to be an incredibly successful first season for the WNBA. The league surpassed everyone's expectations, Lieberman-Cline says, because of "how the league was put together. David Stern and Val Ackerman certainly deserve a pat on the back. They spent a tremendous amount of money to do it right. I was impressed that they treated us like it was a major professional league. Not a girls' league, but a major professional league. And I think that they put the money and promotion behind it. I think people realize that this was not, 'Let's see how the girls do, and if they do OK, we'll stick with it.' When you put forty million dollars behind your league, it says there is a commitment."

Commitment is the word that best describes how Nancy became a basketball icon whose life has been an integral part of women's basketball history for more than two decades.

A trip back to New York City can help show the level of her dedication to basketball.

Life was not easy for Nancy Lieberman in Queens. "We were poor. My father left us. There were days when they were turning off the electricity in the house. We didn't have enough money to put gas in the car. If my grandparents hadn't supported us, we probably would have been on welfare.

"I was angry at my father for not being there. I was angry at my mother for being there. I was just angry. I was mad at everybody. I couldn't understand why I couldn't have my dad at home. I couldn't understand why they were always fighting when they were around."

The streets of New York provide plenty of outlets for angry young people who feel alienated from their families. And for the most part, those outlets don't represent something wholesome and healthy with a vision for the future. Nancy Lieberman, though, chose wisely.

"I turned that energy into basketball," she says. "I would just go to the schoolyards, hang out with the kids, and play basketball. It didn't matter if they were black or white. They liked me. They wanted me to be on their team."

Besides her anger, she also had the stimulus of the New York Knicks. "I was a diehard Knicks fan," she says. "I would watch them on TV, and I decided that was what I wanted to do. I always thought I'd play for the Knicks. I thought they'd need a white girl in the backcourt with Walt Frazier and Earl Monroe. I laugh at it now, but I never thought I wouldn't play for the Knicks."

To hone her basketball skills, Nancy knew she had to play against the best guys in New York, and she heard that the best players were in Harlem. So, when she was thirteen, she began taking the "A" train from Queens to Harlem and showing up at the courts.

As she tells it, she breaks into a bit more of the hard-edged New York accent she used back then. "I'd just walk in and say, 'Who's got next?'

"These black guys would look at me like, 'Who's this?'

"I'd just say, 'Fine. If you don't have next, then I do. And you'll need to see me if you want to play.'

"They just looked at me. They must have been thinking, *Is this girl nuts or is she good?*"

She was good, all right. Good enough at that young age to go up against the likes of Dean Meminger on those playgrounds. Later, it was Meminger who played at Madison Square Garden for Nancy's beloved Knicks.

As Lieberman built up her reputation on the playgrounds as a star basketball player, her mom wished for something far different. The daughter of parents who were in show business as vaudeville performers and having grown up with Beverly Sills, Renee Lieberman was not into sports. She wanted her daughter to be the queen of the ball while Nancy wanted to be the queen of basketball. At one point after her mom had tried again to talk her out of spending all her time on sports, Nancy looked her mom in the eye and announced, "Someday I'm going to make history."

When Nancy was a sophomore at Far Rockaway High, she began playing basketball against girls. Making history was not far behind. That year, the Far Rockaway Seahorses lost the championship game of the city league by one point. In her junior year, the Seahorses lost Nancy.

"There was this rule that was kind of out there that said you couldn't play in the Catholic Youth Organization while playing in high school. We only played fourteen or fifteen games at Far Rockaway, and it wasn't enough for me. I wanted to play more. There were a lot of kids who played both high school and CYO.

"So in my junior year, they asked me to play for St. Francis DeSalles, so I did. Halfway through my junior season, our coach, Brian Sackrowitz, gets on the bus and says, 'Ladies, Nancy has been suspended for playing in the CYO league.'

"I'm sitting there thinking, *You've got to be kidding!* Because people knew of me, all of a sudden the other high schools complained, and this rule was enforced. I just wanted to play. I couldn't get enough of basketball."

In addition to her high school play and her CYO play, Nancy also began to participate in international basketball. In 1974 she played on the US national team, and in 1976, she traveled to Montreal to play on the US Olympic team.

It makes sense that Lieberman-Cline feels that the Olympic experience is her career highlight in basketball. After all, she made history that year by being the youngest Olympic basketball player ever to win a medal as the US captured the silver, finishing second behind the Soviet Union.

"Being on the Olympic team was special," Nancy says. "Especially the first time. I was a senior in high school, and I was so young. It's incredible to play for your country. It's one of the most selfless things you can do. You try out for yourself, but you then play for your country, and I think that's the greatest honor you can have as an athlete."

Something else was going on in Montreal that year—something that anyone who lived through the '70s with an eye on the Olympics can never forget. The Montreal Games was the first test of the Olympic movement since the tragic murders of several members of the Israeli team in the 1972 Games in Germany.

"It was a pretty tough Olympics because it was right after Munich," Nancy recalls. "There was a lot of sadness and a lot of trepidation. I really think people didn't know what to expect. Tight security made it rather difficult to get around. We never really said it, but I think we were all a little nervous."

Fortunately, the Games went off unhindered by political terrorism. In 1980, politics again entered into the picture when the US chose to boycott the Olympics in Moscow. Lieberman was one of the disappointed members of the US team that had their hearts set on defeating the Soviets in basketball in their own backyard.

In the meantime, back in the USA, Nancy had carved out a successful career at Old Dominion University. Because she played in the days before women's college basketball had left the old Association of Intercollegiate Athletics for Women (AIAW) in favor of the NCAA, there was very little in the way of rules for recruiters. It was rare that a college spent much time or money on recruitment for women's college basketball anyway.

Nancy's situation began to change that. "When I was being recruited, it was a strange time in athletics," Nancy says. "There weren't any five-visit rules, but nobody had money to bring you in anyway. You had to go on who had the nicest brochure or the best letterhead." She's only partly kidding.

Lieberman had been hotly pursued by many colleges long before her senior year at Far Rockaway. She had more than 100 scholarship offers, yet she had no help in knowing what to do. "I had no one to protect me. It was open season." Because her relationship with her mom was still strained, she was left to make up her own mind.

One option was to go to Cal-State, Fullerton, where her 1976

Olympic coach, Billie Moore, had the clipboard. But Nancy was afraid Moore would leave the program and strand the New York girl in California.

But then finally, Old Dominion came on the scene. The Virginia school had something in its favor that usually does not make a good recruiting school. It was an unknown. "I wanted a program that no one had ever heard of," Nancy says. "I wanted to be a part of something on the rise. I always considered myself an underdog. I wanted to be part of building something instead of going to an established team like UCLA."

So, Old Dominion acquired the services of the best player in the land, and Nancy took off for Norfolk, Virginia, which she says was "far enough from home that I could get out of New York and grow up, and close enough so that if I got scared, I could go home."

Nancy Lieberman scared? It doesn't seem likely.

In Nancy's first year at ODU, she had an encounter that had little effect on her life at first, but that brought big benefits later. It started when the Athletes in Action men's basketball team paid a visit to the ODU campus.

"I went to watch them shoot around a couple of hours before the game. I was just sitting there on the bench, and Ralph Drollinger [who had played at UCLA and later signed with the Dallas Mavericks] came over to me and introduced himself.

"He said, 'Do you know anything about Christianity or Jesus?'

"I said, 'No, but one of my teammates, Nancy Dunkle, always had a Bible.' "

Nancy had known Dunkle as an Olympian and now with ODU. "I would walk by her room and I'd say, 'What are you doing?' and she would say, 'I'm reading the Bible.' And I'd say, 'What book is that?' She'd talk about Jesus and I'd say, 'What did He do?' " That was the extent of Lieberman's introduction to Christianity until Drollinger sat down beside her.

"I knew I was missing something in my life. Ralph asked me if I had ever asked Jesus into my life."

"I said, 'No, how do you do that?'

"He said, 'Well, say this prayer.' And I did, because I wanted something in my life." He had her confess to Christ that she was a sinner and tell Him that she believed that only He could forgive her sins through His death on the cross. But beyond the time of talking and praying, Drollinger had no opportunity to do follow-up with the young believer.

"Here I was, someone who wanted to be a Christian and didn't know how, so I say this prayer. Ralph is with me for this twenty or thirty minutes that we talk about Christ, and then I'm by myself. I had nobody to take me to that next step. Although I was technically a Christian, I didn't know what to do. I was afraid to go to somebody."

It was an awkward time for Nancy. She was embarrassed to ask questions, even of Nancy Dunkle, because she knew so little. And besides, she was Jewish and had no idea how to answer questions about that if someone were to ask. She says, "I didn't know the answers and I didn't want anyone to know that I didn't know the answers."

A couple of years later, another incident shook this already shaky foundation.

"There was a gal who was like a missionary at Virginia Tech. I had gone over there to play a game and she came up to talk to me. She's one of these real aggressive, self-righteous Christians who scare you. When she talked to me, I said I was a Christian. She said, 'Well, God wants you to go to a retreat,' and she told me the date of it. 'And He wants you to grow in the Lord.'

"I said, 'He does?'

"She said, 'Yeah.'

"I said, 'Well, that retreat is during the regional finals.'

"She said, 'God wants you to miss the regional finals and go on this retreat. You need to go see your coach and tell your coach this.' I was so scared. She scared me so much. I just regressed after that. I thought, *If this is what God does, He's scaring me. I don't think I should be scared.*"

For the next ten years or so, there was no growth in Nancy's life.

She conquered the world of basketball, playing in the Women's Basketball League for the Dallas Diamonds, moving on to play for two years in the men's United States Basketball League, and touring for a couple of years with the Washington Generals as they faced the Harlem Globetrotters night after night.

She even met and married her husband through the stint with the Generals. "I always tell people that Tim and I were so depressed from losing two hundred games in a row to the Globetrotters that we decided, 'Let's do something good. Let's get married.' " They were married on May 18, 1988.

It was not until two years later that both Tim and Nancy began to grow as Christians. Nancy's dormant faith had not been nurtured, and she knew very little about the Word of God. That began to change when Tim, who was working for the three-on-three tournament Hoop It Up, asked Nancy to go to Omaha to help promote a tournament there.

While in Nebraska, Nancy got to know Dean and Pat Thompson, a strong Christian couple who took her to church with them while she was in town. There, for the first time, she began to hear about Bible doctrine and about the importance of Christian fellowship. The Thompsons' pastor taught a Bible study, and Nancy was soon enthralled by what she was learning.

"I didn't know what the word 'fellowship' meant. I didn't know you could pray and ask forgiveness. It was like going to school. I was really learning about who and what we are as Christians."

Soon Tim was joining Nancy at the studies, and together they began to make spiritual progress.

One area in which her growing love of Bible doctrine and teaching is coming into play is in her role as a mother. "We try to get with TJ and as a family read the Bible together. We want him to become a believer, so we want him to hear about Jesus around the house.

"One day TJ asked, 'Mommy, why did those people kill Jesus?' It was tough explaining it to him, but I try to take it at the right pace for him and for me."

When the explaining gets too tough, Nancy picks up the phone and calls the husband of her good friend Rhonda Blades, who played for the New York Liberty in the first WNBA season. "I'll say, 'Parke, why don't you get on the phone to TJ and explain some things to him.' "

It's been a long and historic path for Nancy Lieberman-Cline—from the playgrounds of New York to the fancy arenas of the WNBA. From the simple prayer as a freshman at ODU to the understanding of complex spiritual truths with the help of some friends.

Along the way she's made history—and now she's getting more involved in learning about the history of her faith.

Q & A WITH NANCY LIEBERMAN-CLINE

Q: *How has the game of basketball changed since you first broke into the pros in the early '80s?*
Nancy Lieberman-Cline: I would say easily the depth. With growing opportunities, I think girls know they can participate. You are seeing so many young girls right now who want to play. I really believe you've got to see it to believe it. The moms, the dads are seeing it, so it's inspiring the young girls to go out, to work a little harder, to pursue their goals, to pursue their dreams. . . . We all need that carrot dangling in front of us, because we want to do better.

Q: *Tell the story of you and TJ and the time-out huddle.*
Nancy: We're playing the playoff game, and we're in the huddle. My little boy is waving to me and giving me the thumbs up, and I give him the thumbs up. Cheryl Miller [the Mercury coach] looks at me like, 'What are you doing?' And I'm thinking, 'Now what was that play you called?' At the most intense moment, it's all in perspective. It was all there for me as an athlete, as a mom, as a wife, and more important, as a Christian.

Q: *What do you think your contribution to basketball has been?*
Nancy: What I didn't have in experience, I made up for in being gifted. I could dunk a tennis ball in high school. I was physical. I wasn't afraid to use my body or throw an elbow. That's probably one of my contributions to basketball. I brought a physicalness— the way men play. A lot of girls didn't like me when I was in high school and college 'cause they thought I was mean. It's the way the game is played today. I'm a very physical player.

THE LIEBERMAN-CLINE FILE

Additional information on Nancy Lieberman-Cline:
Nancy Lieberman-Cline Basketball Camp
P.O. Box 795054
Dallas, TX 75379-5054
Phone 972-612-6090

Book on basketball by Nancy Lieberman-Cline
Basketball for Women
by Nancy Lieberman-Cline and Robin Roberts
USA Coaches Clinic, supplier

Lavonna Martin-Floreal

1992 Olympic Silver Medalist: Track

SURPRISES ALONG THE WAY

VITAL STATISTICS

Born: November 18, 1966, in Dayton, Ohio
Height: 5'6"
College: University of Tennessee
Family: Husband, Edrick; son, Edrick, Jr. (EJ)
Residence: Lexington, Kentucky

CAREER HONORS

All-State soccer player, Trotwood-Madison High School, Dayton, Ohio

Thirteen-time All-American in track at Tennessee

Five-time NCAA Champion at Tennessee

1990: Goodwill Games Bronze medal, 100-meter hurdle

1988, 1992: Member, US Track and Field Olympic team

1992: Olympic Silver medal, 100-meter hurdle

OTHER HIGHLIGHTS

1996: Held Lavonna Martin Invitational track meet, Dayton, Ohio

WARMING UP

Lavonna Martin-Floreal relishes the position she finds herself in as a role model for young black women. "They need to see a person who has commitment," Lavonna says. "I think we don't have enough strong, committed Christians in the black community. The community is strong as far as churches, but not as far as having a strong personal relationship with Jesus. I keep pounding on commitment. This is one way the Lord is using me."

FAVORITE BIBLE PASSAGE

"When I was competing and getting ready for the Olympics, I liked the verse, 'What is impossible with men is possible with God' (Luke 18:27). But now that I'm transitioning out of the sport and into a new phase of life, I depend on Psalm 20:7, which says, 'Some trust in chariots and some in horses, but we trust in the name of the Lord our God.' "

Lavonna Martin-Floreal

Have you ever thought of the many, many factors that have to work together for an athlete to reach the highest levels of success? The way so many events have to line up perfectly for an athlete to be in the position to be one of the best in the world?

A look at the athletic career of Lavonna Martin is a lesson in that aspect of sports. As her story will demonstrate, what you suppose will happen in sports seldom does, and what you never expected to happen is what often takes place.

For Lavonna, a case in point is her experiences before, during, and after the 1992 Olympic Games in Barcelona, Spain.

First, let's look at the Before picture.

The Before picture begins in Dayton, Ohio, in 1957—even before Lavonna was born. Her parents were both athletes and track enthusiasts. In fact, Harold Martin had distinguished himself as a star track athlete at Central State University in Ohio. Lavonna's mother, Brenda, who went to school "in an era when women weren't supposed to be in sports," as Lavonna says, was nonetheless a good athlete.

When Lavonna was old enough to start jumping over things in the Martin home, her father decided to turn that energy into something worthwhile. He started the Northwest Track Club, included Lavonna and her brother, Dwayne, and began to cart the kids around the countryside to compete with other up-and-coming track stars.

As Lavonna continued to improve her track ability, she also played soccer at Trotwood-Madison High School, a school with a good reputation for soccer. Because of Lavonna's speed, she excelled on the pitch. Yet all was not rosy.

"I went to a majority white school, and to be an outstanding black athlete was hard. I was the only black girl on the team, and I was the key player mainly because I could run. I was a sweeper and a stopper. Girls could kick the ball ten or fifteen feet ahead of them; and I would run them down. There was a lot of jealousy on the team because I was All-State, which was unheard of for a black girl."

Lavonna can't single out why that was so, and she doesn't think it was because of her teammates. "I can't say it was the kids on the team; it was just a stigma I've had to grow up with."

Soccer, though, was not to be Lavonna's ticket to athletic greatness. It was back on the track that she really excelled. And it was in track that Lavonna wanted to make her mark.

The reasons were several. First, of course, was her parents' influence. Second, she had heard her parents tell her about the career of track legend Wilma Rudolph, who had captured the gold medal in the 100- and 200-meter dash in the 1960 Olympics in Rome. And third, as a young high school student, she watched as Benita Fitzgerald-Brown defeated fellow countrywoman Kim Turner to take the gold medal at the 1984 Olympic Games in Los Angeles.

Her heroes, it seemed, were all track stars, and Lavonna seemed destined to head that way herself.

Heavily recruited out of high school, Lavonna decided to head for the University of Tennessee. "It was close enough so that my family could come to visit and to watch me compete," she recalls. But that wasn't all. She could have just as easily gone to her dad's alma mater at Central State, which was less than a half-hour from home. After all, her brother ended up going there.

The real reason she went to Tennessee was that the Volunteers had, "at that time," she says, "the top women's school in the nation for track. I had a good rating system that I had put together on each school, and Tennessee was at the top." And, oh yes, that's where Olympic gold medalist Benita Fitzgerald went to school.

So, after taking recruiting visits to UCLA, USC, Arizona, LSU, and Tennessee, Lavonna settled on going to school in Knoxville, where she ran for coach Terri Crawford. Subsequently, Crawford left Tennessee to take another coaching position, but Lavonna hooked up with her again later.

Lavonna knew she was being pursued by a lot of schools when she decided on Tennessee, but it wasn't until she signed with the Volunteers that her dad showed her the mail she had received. More than 100 colleges wanted her to run track for their programs.

While at Tennessee, Martin proved that she belonged at one of the top track programs. For one thing, she was almost a one-woman track team. She competed in several dash events, hurdle events, the mile relay, and the 4 x 100. That explains how she was able to become a thirteen-time All-American at Tennessee.

During her stellar career at Tennessee—she graduated in 1989—she earned the right to compete in the 1988 Olympics in Seoul, Korea. As she looks back on that experience now, a funny thing happens. One might think that an initial Olympic experience—one that places a young star in the elite class among American and world runners—would be the stuff of memories. That Lavonna would love to retell such a story as she savors the fond recollections of being a young woman in a foreign country.

You're not going to hear it.

Lavonna Martin simply doesn't recall much about the 1988 Olympics. "I was just there. I wasn't focused. I was so in love, and my boyfriend was living back in the States. I was so focused on wanting to be with him that I wasn't even thinking about the Olympics. My mom will mention something that happened, and I'll say, 'What? I don't remember it.' " (By the way, the relationship with that boyfriend eventually ended—which is obviously a good thing for her career.)

So, returning to the States without any medals and without even much of a memory of the most important track event so far in her career, Martin set out to restore the fire to her career.

A review of the factors of Lavonna Martin's life would lead one to conclude that despite a less-than-successful 1988 Olympic experience, a bright future still lay ahead.

Lavonna obviously thought so, because after her graduation from Tennessee in 1989, she moved to Texas to concentrate on her training. In Austin, Lavonna worked under the watchful eye of her former college coach Terri Crawford.

"My career was doing well. I was always considered in the top five in the United States in the 100-meter hurdles. I started cracking onto the world scene." From 1989 to 1991, everything was going well as Lavonna bore down on a spot on the 1992 Olympic team.

This time things would be different. Older, more mature, she would be able to focus on the right things. Perhaps she would win the medal her career had seemed to promise.

But then came a factor that she could never have suspected. A factor that was nearly devastating. In January 1991, Martin was accused of taking a steroid derivative—an illegal substance.

"We had to submit to out-of-competition testing, in which they test for steroids, diuretics, and any performance-enhancing agent. I was discovered to have a diuretic in my system, which is used to expel water out of your system. The coach who had given it to me gave it to me with the hopes of helping me lose weight, which is why most women take it. Most women take it in Mydol or Pamprin, to help them relieve water during their cycle. She gave it to me to help me lose weight. I've always had a struggle with my weight." The coach who had done this was not Crawford or Beverly Kearney, another mentor she trusted, but, as Lavonna says, "a Russian coach."

Lavonna was devastated. She had worked hard to get another chance to compete in the Olympics, and now, because of a coach's decision, she was in trouble.

"She gave it to me without my knowledge. According to our rules, it doesn't matter if someone gave you something or even whether you know or didn't know. If it's in your system, you're guilty.

"As a result, I was supposed to be suspended for two years. This happened in January 1991, so I would be out until 1993.

"At the time, my coach was telling me, 'It doesn't matter, you can come back for the 1996 Olympics.' But as an athlete, my focus was to compete at the 1992 Olympics. I had just gone along for the ride in 1988, but now I knew what I needed to do to be an Olympic athlete and possibly win a medal. So my goal was 1992."

Lavonna and those who knew her got set for a battle. They knew she had not done anything wrong. They made up, as Lavonna puts it, "a great support system."

Two other things worked together to help her get out from under the suspension. One was "tremendous prayer and fasting—trusting and believing God." The other was, as Lavonna puts it, "a very good lawyer who happened to be on the law and legislation committee of the athletic congress. He knew the ins and outs of the rules. He knew how we could fight this.

"I was supposed to be suspended for twenty-four months, but I was suspended for only fourteen months." That meant Lavonna could get back into training for the Olympics in March of 1992 with the trials in June.

During those fourteen months, Lavonna attempted to keep training, but her unknown status made it tough to train as she knew she should. "I did stay fit, but I wasn't training at the level I probably needed to. Fortunately, my college coach, Beverly Kearny, welcomed me back in her arms. She took me in and really worked me hard."

At the same time Lavonna was edging her body back into shape for Olympic competition, a similar transformation was beginning in her heart. For years, she had drifted away from the relationship with Jesus Christ that had begun back in Dayton when she was thirteen years old.

In the late '60s and early '70s, Brenda Martin was not a churchgoer, even though she had a church background. She sent Lavonna and her brothers to church, but she never went herself. But then, when Lavonna was about eleven years old, someone introduced Mrs. Martin to the concept of accepting Jesus Christ as Savior and having a personal relationship with Him. Suddenly, she was going with the kids to church, trying to find the right one for them.

With that influence, Lavonna accepted Christ as her Savior when she was thirteen years old. The budding track and soccer star now had a beginning in the Lord, but it never developed. "It never took root," Lavonna says.

For the next ten years or so, Lavonna's life was lukewarm to spiritual things. "I went to church, but I was really judgmental to my friends. I knew so much church talk. I was always judging others. I was living the life I wanted to live, when I wanted to do it, and how I wanted to do it."

It was not a life in which Jesus Christ was at the center. During the time of her suspension, she was trying to go it alone.

"I was living in Austin, Texas, and my mother just about demanded that I come back to Dayton. She felt like I needed family. When I came back, she literally forced me to go to church.

"I didn't want to go, because when you're down and depressed, the last thing you want to do is go to church. I'm thankful that she made me go, because it was in going to church, talking to various ministers, and having people praying for me and rallying behind me, it built me up.

"At that point, I had to make a choice," she says. "Was I going to live or was I going to die? Not physically die, but just spiritually and emotionally, I was dead. At that time, I realized that I had to shape up or else, or my life was going down the tubes. I needed to learn more about what it means to have a personal relationship with Christ."

Lavonna renewed her relationship with Christ, rededicating herself to living for Him as she prepared for the Olympics.

With just a short time to prepare for the trials, Lavonna stepped up her training regimen, and she made the team. "It was the hardest meet I was ever in. Of all those terrific people who were there, there were only three that would make the Olympic team."

To review that year going into the Olympics is to point out again the nature of the unexpected. First, the surprise of being suspended. Second, the pleasant and unpredictable suspension of her suspension. Third, her return to her spiritual roots in time to help her prepare spiritually for the Games.

There was another surprise in store for Lavonna as this story unfolds, but it did not sneak up on her until she arrived in Barcelona.

Remember 1988 when she went to Seoul but her heart was left behind with her boyfriend in the US? For this Olympic trip, Lavonna had no such entanglements. She had no boyfriend, and she had no intention of looking for one.

Her focus was on her growing faith and on her chances of winning a medal. The faith was boosted by a new friend, Madeline Mims, a former Olympic medalist who was serving in Barcelona as a chaplain to the Olympians. "Madeline said she had been praying, asking who God was going to raise up on the track circuit. She said that she had no sooner said that than I came up to her and said, 'Hey, how are you doing?'

"The Lord told her, 'That's her right there,' referring to me," Lavonna says. "Madeline was very instrumental in helping me stay spiritually focused."

As far as Lavonna's medal chances were concerned, she was feeling good there too. "I was on a high just being at the Olympic Games. I had some good things happen for me. There were some top athletes who were not there because of being hurt or having problems with drug testing. I began to think, 'Hey, my chances are great.'"

But then came the surprise of the Olympics.

"When I came back to my room one night, Edrick Floreal was with one of our roommates, just sitting there in my room watching TV. The Canadians didn't have TVs in their rooms, but we did.

"I vaguely remember that he asked me a question, and I didn't like the question he asked me, so I kind of snapped off at him. At that point, he told me later, he wasn't even paying attention to me."

To her surprise, though, she felt that the Lord was giving her a message. "Distinctly, as I walked into that room, I felt God tell me, 'That's your husband.'

"I'm thinking, *Please, I'm not here to meet a man. I'm here to run in the Olympics.*"

Regardless of what she thought of God's prompting or of Edrick's first impression on her, she found more than she had expected in Barcelona.

"In the course of that two-week period, we spent a lot of time together. We went to church together. Madeline was very instrumental in helping me decipher my feelings. Edrick was a very young believer, at about the same stage I was a few months before. I was trying to decide, *Do I want to make a commitment or not?* It was during the last two days that we both realized what was going on. We both realized that we were destined to be together. And believe it or not, during that two-week period was when he asked me to marry him."

Floreal, a Canadian long-jumper, and Martin, an American hurdler, jumped into each other's arms and decided to get married.

"You can imagine how my parents felt!" says Lavonna with a laugh. "I went to the Olympics with no boyfriend, and came out with the person I wanted to marry. They thought I was just caught up in the Olympic glamour."

In the midst of this surprising relationship, Lavonna also had a responsibility to the United States of America. She, along with other runners, carried with her the hopes of the US in the 100-meter hurdles.

To get to the finals at Barcelona, Lavonna had to make it through three rounds of races. "The first three rounds were the best rounds I had ever run. I won all three rounds. I was very focused. It wasn't until I won the third round that I realized, *I can win this*.

"That was a mental mistake. Instead of just staying focused and saying, 'OK, I have just one more round,' I began worrying.

"When I went to the final round, I was so nervous, so scared."

Heading into the race, Lavonna was right where she needed to be physically. Because of her wins, she had one of the choice lanes. Yet the mental stress got to her. "Everyone kept talking about Gail Devers, and I was pretty nervous just having to compete with her. I had never been in the Olympic finals. It was pretty overwhelming."

Despite running what Lavonna calls "really bad for the first few hurdles," she began to pick up speed near the end. She thinks she knows why. "No one can ever tell me that it wasn't the hand of God that I felt push me from behind. When I was at the last hurdle, the race was like a blur, but something propelled me to second place."

Gail Devers wasn't the winner of that race. Devers, who was attempting to capture the gold in both the 100 meters and the 100 meters hurdle, fell after catching her toe on the final hurdle. As she went down, Greece's Paraskivei Patoulidou flashed past Devers to win the gold in 12.64. Right behind Patoulidou was Lavonna, who picked up her silver medal with a time of 12.69.

Lavonna Martin was an Olympic medal winner.

So she went home with a silver and with prospects of getting a diamond. Talk about surprises!

Several months later, Edrick Floreal and Lavonna Martin were married.

In the years since 1992, Lavonna has tried and failed to reclaim Olympic glory. After giving birth to Edrick Jr. in 1995, Lavonna got herself back into shape and made a run at the 1996 Olympic team. However, the day before the trials were to begin, she pulled a muscle in her stomach, an injury that prevented her from making the squad.

More recently, the Floreals have concentrated on Edrick's budding career as a track coach. "Edrick has an outstanding ability as far as coaching goes," Lavonna says. "I'd like to see him take it as far as possible." After serving as assistant coach at Georgia Tech, Floreal moved on to the University of Kentucky, where he was named head track coach for the 1997–98 season.

While Edrick mentors the next generation of athletes, Lavonna contemplates her next move. With a teaching degree from Tennessee and an interest in helping young people, Lavonna seeks God's direction.

As late as the fall of 1997, she was still struggling with letting go of her track career. "I know that God is saying to me, 'I'm your source. I'm your source for everything.' Not long ago, I was still making track my source. I was reading in the book *Experiencing God*, and I felt God was asking me, 'When are you going to yield to Me? When are you going to trust Me?'

"I finally said, 'I'm done, Lord. If you want me to keep working at Target [which she was doing at the time] in order to get me where You want me to be, then I'll just yield.'"

For an athlete who has reached the highest level of success, it's not easy to be willing to stay out of the spotlight and to give up the glamour associated with world-class sports. But if Lavonna Martin-Floreal has learned anything, she has learned that God has plenty more surprises for her as she uses her silver medal status as a witness for Him. The unknown can be frightening for everyone, but Lavonna has seen God work enough in her life to know He can be trusted.

"God knows what He is doing," she says. "I realize that."
That's enough for each of us to know.

Q & A WITH LAVONNA MARTIN-FLOREAL

Q: *What stands out to you about Barcelona?*
Lavonna Martin-Floreal: The mere fact that I was there was a miracle from God. That in itself made it so much more special. I was in a spot where everyone said I'd never be. I just enjoyed my whole time in Barcelona, just basking in the fact that God had performed this great miracle in my life. Also, at this Olympics I met my husband. So that will always stick in my mind.

Q: *What do you think your next career move will be?*
Lavonna: I'm not sure I want to teach, but I want to be involved with youth. I might want to coach at the college level. One thing I've been doing is going into the school systems and tapping into their character education programs. I talk to the kids about character. I can't talk about Jesus, though. But if they invite me to come in and talk about my Olympic experience, I can. I think God can use this. He'll touch whoever needs to be touched.

Q: *What do you do to stay strong spiritually?*
Lavonna: I have started a neighborhood Bible study for women. That keeps me grounded. Also, Edrick and I have found a church in our city that meets both of our needs. We've found out that we're to be in prayer for everything. Prayer helps us stay in the mode God wants us to be in. God's been showing me that He is God, and that it doesn't matter what the world wants to focus on.

Barb Mucha

Professional Golfer

AT THE TOP OF HER GAME

VITAL STATISTICS

Born: December 1, 1961, in Parma, Ohio
Height: 5'6"
College: Attended the University of Cincinnati; graduated from
   Michigan State University
Single
Residence: Orlando, Florida
Special Interests: Bowling, fishing, Christian fellowship

CAREER HONORS

1990: Boston Five Classic
1992: Oldsmobile Classic
1994: State Farm Rail Classic
1996: Chick-fil-A Charity Championship

OTHER HIGHLIGHTS

All-American honorable mention in 1984
Earned more than $300,000 on the LPGA Tour in 1996
Posted a career-low 71.86 scoring average in 1996
Carded her first pro hole-in-one at the 1991 US Open

WARMING UP

Barb Mucha doesn't want the easy way out. In fact, the easy way out for her might be too hard. For instance, she enjoys playing courses "that are a little longer and require demanding shots. That causes me to focus in on my game and work a little harder out there. Sometimes I get a little lazy and lack concentration when the courses aren't challenging. If [I] have too much leeway, I tend to get careless."

FAVORITE BIBLE PASSAGE

Yet this I call to mind and therefore I have hope: Because of the Lord's great love we are not consumed, for his compassions never fail. They are new every morning; great is your faithfulness (Lamentations 3:21–23).

"No matter what is going on, no matter what circumstances, joys, or trials come into my life, God's faithfulness has been a constant factor in my Christian walk. This is something that I'm starting to grasp and understand. God is faithful, no matter how good or bad something seems. His faithfulness is new every day!"

Barb Mucha

Funny how careers go, isn't it?

You work hard at your chosen profession for years, wondering if you are making a mark. You take your gains, you take your losses, and you learn from both.

You watch as an occasional fellow employee rockets to the top of the profession. You notice others who don't quite make it as you pass them on the way.

Yet you plod along—doing your best and hoping you are being appreciated for your accomplishments.

Then suddenly something wonderfully surprising starts to happen. You begin to be considered an expert. Your opinion starts to count. You find others looking up to you.

You begin to realize that you are near the top of your profession. You are one of the best salespeople, auto repairmen, or flight attendants. You have arrived.

That's where Barb Mucha has found herself recently. After more than ten years of hard work on the Ladies' Professional Golfers Association Tour, she finally climbed into the company of the elite.

As the saying goes, it took her ten years to become an overnight success. And it took the words of Barb's golf coach to wake her up to the fact that she was nearing golf's mountaintop.

The road had been long. It had often been frustrating. And it was paved with stories of both good times and bad times on the golf courses of the Ladies' Professional Golfers Association.

But it led to a remarkable revelation for Mucha in late 1996.

Earlier in the year, in April, Mucha had captured the fourth first place of her career when she won the Chick-fil-A Charity Championship at Eagle's Landing Country Club in Stockbridge, Georgia. On a sunny, warm spring Sunday, Barb held off a charge by Liselotte Neumann to capture the tournament by two strokes.

Despite that victory, Mucha did not consider herself to be one of the top golfers in the game.

After all, in 1995, she had finished forty-second on the money list. Her best finish before that was twenty-third way back in 1990. Good. Very good. After all, to be forty-second best at anything in the country is nothing to be ashamed of.

But things began to take on a whole different perspective as 1996 wound down and Mucha found herself highly rated on the money list (she finished the year fifteenth). That's when Leo Zampedro, Mucha's golf coach since she was ten years old, said something that helped her take her game to a whole new level.

He told his protégé, "You know, Barb, you have arrived. You are there. You are one of the best golfers out there."

Barb Mucha is not an ego-driven person. So this statement was a bit hard for her to accept. "I've given this a lot of thought," she says. "I decided, *Yeah, I'm a good player, but to think I'm one of the best—one of the top players out there*—I began to think that was too arrogant. When someone who has seen your talent and has watched your progress and has coached you for twenty-five years says you've arrived, you are there. Instead of continuing to strive for that place, you are already at that place. So I decided to just perform and allow myself to enjoy where I was.

"Certain weeks you're going to play better than others, but to know in your heart and your head that you're one of the best out there, you don't have to prove yourself anymore."

In a funny kind of way, Barb Mucha has been proving herself on the golf course most of her life.

To begin, she had to prove to herself that the game was even enough fun to play. As a nine-year-old self-described tomboy growing up in Parma Heights, Ohio, she found herself out on the links with her father and uncle—and not enjoying her time in nature.

"They would go play nine holes," she says, "and I would go

with them. But I didn't enjoy it. I didn't like it because I wasn't very good."

She probably would rather have been bowling. After all, that was her first love. Or playing basketball. She liked that. Or even dinking around with a volleyball.

But not golf. "The other sports, I knew how to play them. But with golf, it was like anything else: If you don't know what you are doing, you struggle with it."

The struggle didn't last long, though. Despite her first impressions of golf, it wasn't long until she had caught on well enough to make some noise in the sport.

When she was ten, Barb entered a junior golf tournament sponsored by a Cleveland newspaper. Entering tournaments was nothing new—she had competed in bowling contests. This time, though, something happened that changed everything.

She won. "I got a three-and-a-half-foot trophy," she recalls. "I think that had a big influence on me. My picture was in the paper, and they had articles about me. That kind of told me, if I can win, I ought to keep playing."

There was one problem. Barb still did not like golf.

That would all change very soon. Barb's parents saw enough potential in their reluctant linkster to employ the services of a local club pro to coach her. That man was Leo Zampedro, the man who many years later told Barb that she should consider herself among golf's elite. He not only taught her how to play, but he also convinced her that she could enjoy golf. "If you get instruction and learn, you begin to like it," Mucha says.

She took her growing love for golf to Valley Forge High School, where she played on the boys' golf team because the school didn't have a team for the girls. "The guys weren't keen on having a girl playing golf with them. But after a couple of matches, they accepted me. By the time I was a senior, I was playing first or second. I got respect from the guys."

She wasn't a one-sport person, though. "I enjoyed basketball. I was pretty good. I was a point guard, and my strength was foul shots. I hit 75 to 80 percent of those."

Besides sports, Mucha also excelled in the classroom, where she maintained a grade point average near 4.0 and was declared the Business Student of the Year in her senior year.

As good as she was in golf, though, she wasn't recruited by any colleges, so she was on her own to find the college of her choice. "I didn't want to go far away. I wanted to stay in Ohio." Her search led her south to Cincinnati, where she enrolled at the University of Cincinnati.

"The golf coach there, Carol Johnson, was a wonderful person." She selected Mucha to be a part of the team and helped the continuing education that transformed Barb from a reluctant golfer to one who was serious about her game. "I wasn't a bad student. I went to class and got good grades, but my main focus back then was to go to practice. I wanted to learn as much about the game as I possibly could."

Just as she was getting comfortable with Cincinnati and its golf program, Mucha encountered a drastic change. The university was facing some budgeting problems and decided to drop the golf program.

"I didn't want to start all over again. I didn't want to go to a new school." But if she wanted to pursue golf, she didn't have any choice.

Upon the recommendation of her coach and despite the fact that the new school was not in any position to recruit her, Mucha traveled north to East Lansing, Michigan, and entered Michigan State University, where she played for coach Mary Fossum. As nice a school as MSU is, it certainly had its share of drawbacks for a young golfer.

For one, "It's not good golfing weather," Mucha admits. "We practiced a lot indoors. A lot of times we were out in miserable, wet weather—practicing. After all is said and done, though, it turned out to be a good decision."

The details bear this out. As a senior, Mucha was selected as the Spartans' Most Valuable Player, and she was named All-American, honorable mention. She led the team with a 78.10 average over thirty-nine rounds of golf. In the NCAA championships, Mucha led all of the Spartan players with a 309 for 72 holes to finish twenty-first in the country.

In the process of leading the team in her senior year, Mucha captured three titles: the Illinois State Invitational, the Wolverine Invitational, and the Ohio State Invitational. There was a sweet irony in that last championship, for it was to Ohio State that a lot of the top players traditionally went—the golfers who were recruited out of high school, and the golfers who were chosen four years earlier when Barb was passed by in the recruiting game.

Upon graduating from Michigan State with a degree in personnel administration, Mucha felt her next step should be the pros. After all, she says, "Every time I went to a tournament [in college] I got better. I thought I should give it a shot and see what I could do."

Every professional athlete has an idea of what should happen as he or she begins to take those first steps toward earning a living in sports. For most, those steps include more than the things we generally think of as related to athletics. Sometimes there are decisions to make about other people. Often there are financial considerations to take into account. Sometimes—and this was the case for Barb Mucha—a spiritual situation stands between her and her first ventures out into the world of pro golf.

Growing up, Mucha had attended church. She had listened as the preacher spoke. And at Michigan State, she had attended Fellowship of Christian Athletes meetings and had found them beneficial. Yet despite these positive responses to Christian situations, a key element was missing. "I didn't really know it was a personal relationship with Jesus Christ that I needed. I didn't know about the one-to-one relationship."

That all changed in 1984, a few months after Barb graduated from Michigan State. "I had been going to church with my brother and his wife for a long time. But one day when I was there, the pastor was speaking from the book of John. He was telling us that Jesus was the light of the world. When he was done preaching, he asked everyone to bow in prayer, and he asked us to pray.

"I felt that God was drawing me. It was like I could see in my mind a tunnel with a bright light at the end. God was saying, 'I am the light.' At that time, I accepted Jesus Christ as my Savior. It was December 1984."

Equipped with her new faith, Barb Mucha set off to seek her fortune in pro golf. During the next two years, she toiled on the Futures Tour—far from the apparent glamour of the LPGA Tour. During her time on the Futures, Mucha won six tournaments, proving that she was an up and coming golfer. Beyond that, she says, it was a spiritual training period. "God was preparing me before I began the Tour," she says of those two seasons.

The next step for a pro golfer is to qualify for the big Tour—to get a "card." For Mucha, the moment of truth came on the week of October 14 through 17, 1986, at the Sweetwater Country Club in Sugar Land, Texas. During those three days, she shot a 72-hole total of 311 to make the Tour as a nonexempt qualifier. Six weeks before her twenty-fifth birthday, Barb Mucha finally achieved what sixteen years of practice and tutelage under Leo Zampedro earned for her: a chance to play on the LPGA Tour.

What more could a young woman want? Fame. Money. The thrill of going head-to-head against the best in the game. TV. Sponsors. The excitement of top-flight competition. Surely 1987 would be the highlight of Barb Mucha's life. The apex of a career in golf. A joyous excursion through pro golf.

Well, maybe not.

"I hated my first year on tour," Barb says in her typical honest, straightforward way. "I just hated it. I didn't know anyone."

What's worse, the fact that she was a nonexempt qualifier meant that she was a conditional player. Each Monday, she had to qualify for the event of the week. And even then she wasn't sure until the last minute that she would be playing on Thursday.

Mucha's Michigan State golf coach Mary Fossum puts into perspective what Mucha discovered in her first year going up against pros such as Nancy Lopez, Betsy King, and Laura Davies instead of college students from Northwestern, Purdue, and Illinois. "It's a great experience, but it's not as easy as people think. It's a dog-eat-dog situation."

Speaking of dogs, Mucha probably subsisted on hot dogs during that first year out; she earned a scant $6,657 in 1987—hardly enough for bus fare to the fifteen tournaments she competed in. She finished behind 139 other golfers in her rookie season. That sent her back to square one. She didn't make enough money or finish high enough in the rankings to get an exemption for 1988, and she failed to qualify at the 1987 Qualifying Tournament back down in Sugar Land, Texas.

"I was pretty devastated," Mucha says about the turn of

events. "I didn't feel like I was as good as a lot of people I was play-ing with. I had talked myself out of believing it could get better."

But Mucha had something in her favor that even a bad year on the Tour couldn't negate. It shows through in the words of Coach Fossum, who described Mucha as "a great competitor who can handle pressure well." That competitive nature came to the fore-front in 1988 when the young golfer faced a possible future with-out pro golf.

She took some time off, regrouped, and set out to resurrect her game. Along to help in the reconstruction project was a new coach, Suellen Northrup. The two of them decided that there was a flaw in her swing that would hinder her on the Tour. So, they dis-mantled her swing and revamped it. Northrup combined the new swing with a new attitude for the game and send Mucha back out on the Futures Tour to put the changes into practice.

After that season ended, Mucha journeyed again to Sugar Land for Q school, where this time she qualified with a 308—three strokes better than her 1986 qualifying score.

A few strokes per competition may not sound like much, but for Mucha the really important number of strokes turned out to be two. That is how many strokes she improved her game between 1987 during her rookie year and 1989 when she made the Tour for good.

Indeed, that two-stroke difference (74.84 average in 1987; 72.88 average in 1989) meant these improvements: Earnings in 1989: $47,849; ranking in 1989: 60.

Hard work and perseverance had paid off. "I had to really grind it out," explains Mucha.

If 1989 was good, 1990 was great.

In one tournament in August 1990, Mucha won almost as much money as she had won in 1987 and 1989 combined. It was the Boston Five Classic at the Tara Ferncroft Country Club in Dan-vers, Massachusetts. Her 11 under par 277 earned her a first-place tie. Her playoff victory over Lenore Rittenhouse gave her a check for $52,500. And it gave her the first true indication that she not only belonged on the Tour, but she had the stuff to be one of the best.

It was, for Barb Mucha, the entrance ramp to the road to the top.

She was twenty-eight years old now and six years removed from a promising college career, but now she had that coveted first win. She had the honor of knowing for the rest of her life that she was the best golfer in the United States on that particular day.

"It was not a shocker," she recalls of the win, "but it was something that you kind of shake your head and say, 'Did this really happen?' That's what you strive for—to try to win a tournament. And to know that you have succeeded is pretty special. You always think you're good enough to win, but when you do there's a lot of emotions going on. There's joy. There's happiness. You're elated. You know how hard it was to get there, and when you win, it kind of brings the whole picture together for you."

Over the next six years, Mucha won a total of four tournaments. But none of them compares with the one she captured on May 31, 1992.

The site was the Walnut Hills Country Club. The tournament was the Oldsmobile Classic. The city was the home of her alma mater, Michigan State University.

In front of an appreciative home crowd, Mucha captured the tournament and the $75,000 first prize. "That was very special. It was the first year they had the tournament, and because I was an MSU graduate, they really wanted me to win the tournament. The support of the people was great."

That wasn't all that was good about 1992. That year Mucha won the most money in her career up to then and finished twenty-seventh on the money list. She was beginning to edge her way toward the top.

The climb slowed somewhat over the next three years as she stayed pretty much in the top fifty but not anywhere near the top twenty-five. She had another victory in 1994 at the State Farm Rail Classic. But there was nothing to indicate that Mucha would break into the elite top fifteen or so of women's golf.

That's why 1996 was such an important year for her. Look at what she did that year:

- Won more than $300,000
- Accumulated five Top 10 finishes
- Crossed the $1 million plateau in career winnings

- Lowered her average to 71.86
- Captured her fourth tournament, the Chick-fil-A Charity Championship

When the tallies were all in and the totals were added up for 1996, Mucha had finished fifteenth on the LPGA Tour. Just like that, she was one of the best in the game. Four times she had been the absolute best for the weekend, and it was time for her to assert her claim as one of the top players in the game.

Leo Zampedro made no apologies for helping Mucha understand what she had achieved. And now, after all she has gone through to get where she is, she can talk freely about what she has accomplished.

Yet this is not about an athlete who has suddenly become an ego-driven prima donna. Instead, it's about an athlete who has used her God-given ability to its peak potential and is thankful for what she has been able to accomplish.

"In a sport like this, which is so individual and so competitive, I want to have that attitude that I'm as good as anybody else—but not that I'm better as a person. I want to balance those two and be happy when other people win. You have to know in your heart that you are there because you worked at it—not because you think you are better than anybody else."

Besides the advice of her golf coach, Mucha also depends greatly on the wisdom she gets from the Bible and from Christian fellowship on tour. In that regard, Cris Stevens, a woman who travels with the LPGA golfers and organizes Bible studies for the women, provides a lot of assistance. "We get into small groups and have some great discussions. Also we pray together. We have some newer Christians in the groups, and I try to share what God has shown me over the years and what He has taught me. It's a bit of a leadership role."

For a golfer who has climbed to a leadership role on the course, it only seems fitting that she adopts a leadership role off it as well.

Another responsibility of leadership that Mucha has taken on is in speaking to youngsters whenever possible. "I make the point to them that God is very real. I know He has touched my life. If you ask Jesus to come into your life, He will manifest Himself.

"I like to tell them that God is faithful. I say that you might not see it now, but maybe two years from now the picture will come together.

"I know that God has never allowed me to slip out of His hand. I may try to jump out, but He's always there to scoop me back up. I know that God has touched my life, and when I start sharing that, they can tell it is sincere."

Another good year in 1997 kept Barb Mucha's name among the leaders on the LPGA money list, hovering for most of the year from tenth to fifteenth on the list. In addition, Mucha was in the Top 10 among LPGA golfers in scoring average, hitting the greens in regulation, and in the number of Top 10 finishes throughout the year.

Two other indications of Mucha's arrival was her spot in the $1.8 million Gillette Tour Challenge Championship, which she earned through her play throughout the season.

She was also in the Top 10 in Solheim Cup standings for most of the season. Without a doubt, Barb Mucha had made good on the words of her coach, Leo, who told her she had arrived on the LPGA Tour.

"When it's all said and done," Mucha concludes. "I want to be remembered as one of the best players out there, but I also want to be remembered as someone who was caring and gave time to other people when they were having rough times. I don't want to receive the credit. I want them to say that it's because of her faith in Christ that she was that way."

Q & A WITH BARB MUCHA

Q: *What is your favorite LPGA tournament?*
Barb Mucha: I'd say it's the Dinah Shore Tournament, which is one of the majors. It's just beautiful out there, and you get the really big crowds. It is very prestigious.

Q: *What kind of course do you play best?*
Barb: I like the courses that are a little longer and that require demanding shots. That causes me to focus in on my game and

work a little harder out there. Sometimes I get a little lazy or have a lack of concentration when the courses aren't challenging. I always enjoy the US Open, because it's always a difficult course.

Q: *You like listening to Christian music. What is it about music that helps you?*
Barb: I've got tons of Christian music. I think I have about eighty CDs. Sometimes when I'm not excited about the Lord, I can turn those on and let the Lord be magnified. The songs remind me how great He is. Of course, I travel a lot, and the CDs help me pass the time. You can saturate your mind with the Word of God in song. When I listen to music, I tend to listen to the words and take it to heart. I especially like Kathy Troccoli, Steve Camp, the Imperials, and ballads.

Q: *What sport would you pursue professionally if you weren't a golfer?*
Barb: Pro bowling. I would like to mess around with it and see what I could do. I think I could be very good at it. If the women are competing on the bowling tour where I'm playing, I'll go see them bowl. Sometimes I tell people I want to try pro bowling, but I'm really trying to focus on my golf. I don't want to make a fool of myself in bowling.

THE MUCHA FILE

LPGA Record

Year	Number of tourneys	Best finish	Money	Rank	Average strokes
1987	15	T21	$6,657	140	74.84
1988	Did not play on LPGA Tour				
1989	18	T5	$47,849	60	72.88
1990	29	1	$149,972	23	72.82
1991	25	T4	$54,085	83	73.55
1992	26	1	$190,519	27	72.57
1993	23	T6	$91,806	56	72.56
1994	25	1	$152,685	36	73.05
1995	25	T2	$156,527	42	72.65
1996	27	1	$304,805	15	71.86
1997	24	3	$309,684	23	71.40

Charlotte Smith

ABL Basketball

HIS WILL, NOT MINE

VITAL STATISTICS

Born: August 23, 1973
Height: 6'0"
College: University of North Carolina
Single
Residence: San Jose, California
Special Interests: Shopping, playing the piano, gospel music

CAREER HONORS

1994: MVP NCAA Final Four
1994, 1995: MVP ACC Tournament
1995: Kodak All-American
1996: Gold medalist, Jones Cup

OTHER HIGHLIGHTS

1995: Named MVP of the Italian League All-Star Game
Third-round draft choice of the Colorado Xplosion
1996: Second-leading scorer and rebounder on Xplosion
December 1994: The first woman in college basketball to execute a
dunk in a game since 1984

WARMING UP

Before Charlotte Smith established herself as a star in her own right, she was known as David Thompson's niece. Thompson, who had a storied career at North Carolina State, including an NCAA championship and Player of the Year honors, was on his way to an incredible pro career when drugs and other problems tripped him up. Later, Thompson became a strong Christian spokesman and an advocate for drug-free living. "I learned a lot about life from my uncle," Charlotte says. "I learned from the things he had to deal with. He was an overcomer."

FAVORITE BIBLE PASSAGE

I can do everything through him who gives me strength (Philippians 4:13).

Charlotte Smith

L ife looked fresh and bright and new for Charlotte Smith in
September 1996. A sparkling college basketball career and a
one-year learning experience in Italy had landed her a prime
spot as one of the founding sisters of the brand-new American Basketball League.

As the popularity of women's basketball continued to take
off, the people who founded the ABL were able to claim the first
salvo in what has become a battle for supremacy in women's pro
hoops. By putting their league together for the fall and winter of
1996, they were able to snag some of the top players available
while also introducing their teams long before the WNBA could
get off the ground.

Taking advantage of this fresh opportunity, Charlotte Smith
began to prepare for her first season. She would be joining North
Carolina teammate Sylvia Crawley and a host of American college
and European pro stars to play for coach Sheryl Estes on the Colorado Xplosion.

"I'm glad to be back at home," Smith said at the time. "I
missed my family while playing overseas."

Smith and former Florida star Tammy Jackson had played
together on the same team in the Italian League the year before.
"Athletically, it was a positive experience for me," she says about
that year in Italy. "I got a chance to better myself as a player. I got to

play out on the perimeter. That helped me take my game to another level."

But there were disadvantages of Italian hoops. "Socially, it was hard. I didn't speak the language. It's hard to get out and do anything if you don't know the language. Plus, there was no church to go to, so that was hard."

But she turned some of the disadvantage into an advantage. Without the distractions of the usual off-the-court life of a pro athlete, Charlotte had more time for more valuable pursuits. "I decided that one of my goals was to read the whole Bible by the end of the season, and I did it!" Plus she had the assistance of Jackson, who, Charlotte says, "helped me keep a level head. She was a Christian, so we read the Bible together. Through the hard times we helped each other hang in there."

When Smith returned to the US and embarked on her career with the Xplosion, though, she did not put the hard times behind her.

With enthusiasm, Charlotte packed up and left North Carolina for Colorado. Along with her to help her settle into her new home was her mom, Etta Smith.

As the Smiths made their way to Colorado, Mrs. Smith became ill. "She had trouble breathing," Charlotte recalls. "She thought it was just heartburn or something like that."

Once Charlotte and her mom had arrived in Denver and had begun to get Charlotte settled in, Etta was still having trouble. "A couple of days after she was in Colorado, she went to the emergency room at the hospital. They discovered that she had double pneumonia." By the time doctors began to treat Mrs. Smith, the illness had affected other organs of her body. A few days after she was admitted to the hospital, Etta Smith died.

"That was the hardest thing that I ever had to deal with," says Charlotte. "I could never imagine that my mom would pass away at such an early age. She had never been sick. She never had anything wrong with her."

For Charlotte, it was a test of faith.

She had been a Christian since she was about fifteen years old. Growing up in a family in which her father, Ulysses Smith, was a pastor, she was never far from the church and the gospel was no mystery to her. But it had been her grandmother who had been instrumental in leading Charlotte to faith in Jesus Christ.

"My grandmother always used to tell us, 'It's time to get your house in order. You never know when Jesus is coming back.' She was always talking about heaven and hell, telling us that in hell we would burn forever. She would tell us that we as humans are not perfect—that we are bound in sin. But God is a forgiving God, she would say."

Charlotte knew her grandmother was right. Even though the teenager was not the kind to get into trouble, at fifteen she understood the need to take care of her sin. "It was a matter of saying, 'Lord, I'm sorry I'm a sinner. Please forgive me. I trust You, Jesus. Please come into my life.' "

So, for the eight years between that day in Shelby, North Carolina, and the time of her mother's death, Charlotte never wavered from her faith in God through Jesus Christ.

Understandably, though, she was shaken by this unfathomable incident. Her mother was gone. Where was God?

"The hardest thing was knowing what God was doing," Charlotte says now. "I didn't understand. For a while, I was just angry with God. 'Why did You take my mom away?' I would ask. We needed her.

"That has been the hardest point in my walk with God," Charlotte says. "I just totally didn't want to open my Bible or pray or anything. I didn't think it was fair for Him to take my mom. It took a while for me to get back on track."

The healing process for the young basketball star was gradual. No great words of wisdom restored her. There was no flash of brilliance from a fellow believer. "I didn't really open up to anyone," Charlotte says. "I didn't think anyone knew how much I was struggling or what I was dealing with in my walk with God."

As the months wore on, though, Charlotte began to see her life return to a bit of normalcy. "I guess time took away some of the pain, and I was able to accept it and move on."

She has finally concluded, as she has had to do in other disappointments in her life, that "everything happens for a reason. I try not to question everything, but let God have His way."

She says, "With the death of my mom, if you look at it from a carnal mind, you really don't understand it. You just have to say, 'God, let Your will be done.' "

Although no other disappointment can come close to losing a loved one, throughout her career Charlotte has learned that the same way of thinking helps a person deal with every difficulty, no matter how big or how small.

One example happened on the basketball court in the time between Charlotte's stellar career at North Carolina and her introduction to the ABL. For several years she had been playing with USA Basketball—the organization that chooses the Olympic team. Yet when it came time for the team to issue invitations for tryouts for the 1996 Olympics, Charlotte did not receive one.

"I had been with USA Basketball since high school and had played internationally in the World University Games. When I observed the invitees, I saw some players who didn't make the Jones Cup teams [another international competition] that I made. There were players who weren't All-Americans. Just from looking at that, I didn't understand."

She may not have understood the situation, but she learned. First, she learned that disappointment can be a catalyst to make her want to improve. "That situation made my desire to be a better player grow even more." And second, she learned another lesson in trusting God. "I saw again that everything happens for a reason. I had to say, 'Whatever God's will is, let it be done.' "

But enough about disappointments. Charlotte Smith is not one who dwells on them, so it wouldn't be fair to dwell on them in her story. Instead, it is perhaps better to turn to what so far has been the crowning achievement of her basketball career. It's an event and a circumstance that few athletes will ever enjoy—a singularly spectacular event that solidifies the athlete's place in sports history.

In baseball, fans remember Joe Carter for his ninth-inning, game-winning 1993 home run that propelled the Toronto Blue Jays to victory in the World Series.

In men's basketball, fans remember Keith Smart for his jump shot that made national champions out of the Indiana Hoosiers in 1985.

In football, Jim O'Brien's field goal in the waning seconds of

Super Bowl V in 1972 made winners of the Baltimore Colts.

And in women's college basketball history, perhaps the single most important and dramatic play of all time was Charlotte Smith's unbelievable three-point basket that gave the North Carolina Tar Heels its first national championship in women's basketball in 1994. For a school that had become accustomed to winning the NCAA crown in men's hoops, Charlotte's shot opened a grand new era in sports history.

It was Sunday, March 30, 1994. The Richmond Coliseum was jammed to the rafters to see whether Louisiana Tech or North Carolina would be the 1994 national champions. As the teams battled their way toward the final gun, the championship was very much up for grabs. With fourteen seconds left, Tech's senior guard Pam Thomas nailed a jumpshot to put the Lady Techsters on top 59-57.

The Tar Heels brought the ball down court and worked it inside to Tonya Sampson, who missed a layup. The battle for the rebound was tied up, and the refs blew the whistle at .7 seconds left on the clock. The possession arrow was pointing North Carolina's way. They would get the ball out of bounds under their basket with less than a second to play.

Tar Heel coach Sylvia Hatchell called a time out to set up a play. She planned to get Crawley the ball under the basket for the tie. But when the team went out to set up, they had trouble getting the ball inbounds, and Stephanie Lawrence called another time out. This time, Hatchell told her players they were going for the win.

When Charlotte heard that in the huddle, she was certain the ball would not go to her. "I didn't think that would include me because I was not the best three-point shooter on the team." Indeed, during her years at North Carolina, Smith hit just 26 percent of her trey attempts.

Yet coaches have to follow their hunches, and Hatchell had a feeling about Charlotte.

The next few seconds were a real mental test for Charlotte. "Before we went out to execute the play, I was thinking, *There's only .7 seconds on the clock. That's hardly time to get a shot off.*"

Smith, the Tech people knew, was a rebounder. She had already grabbed twenty-three for the game, setting a championship-game record. Who would think that a woman who worked the inside so well was a threat from twenty-two feet?

Tech certainly didn't. While they busily guarded Sampson, who broke down the middle as a decoy, Smith sneaked around a Crawley screen unguarded. Lawrence fired a perfect inbounds pass to Charlotte, who grabbed and launched the most dramatic shot in women's college basketball history.

When it hit the net, Smith was engulfed in a mob of white and Carolina blue. The Tar Heels had their first national title. Smith broke into tears of ecstasy as the team congratulated her and tried on their caps that said "1994 NCAA Champions" with the Tar Heels' intertwined NC prominently displayed.

"I was in shock," Charlotte recalls. "I was totally overjoyed. I thought at the time, *God does answer prayers.* That's what I was doing the whole time. Praying that the shot would go in."

"It was just a great accomplishment, not only for me individually but for the university," Charlotte says as she reflects on that title. "We had never won a national championship in women's basketball. We had never won a conference championship. It let me know that you should never give up, and that hard work always pays off. We put in a lot of hard work to build our program up to a national caliber program, so it's just good to know that all that hard work paid off. Perseverance and patience paid off."

Just for Charlotte to be at the University of North Carolina was a testament to patience and perseverance.

There was never any doubt that she would be a top athlete. Growing up in Shelby, North Carolina, she established herself at a young age as one of the best basketball players in the most important arena—in her family. The competition was stiff as she and her two brothers, along with their cousins, met in the backyard of their grandmother's house and went at it. Most of Charlotte's cousins were boys, so she spent countless backyard hours playing against the boys. "On my mom's side of the family I have one girl cousin, but she wasn't interested in basketball. I was the only girl out there playing all my cousins and brothers."

The talent was there and the training was there, but a few obstacles stood between Charlotte and a major college basketball career.

The first was that she was multi-talented, and her number one sport at the outset of her high school career was track. "I ran the mile, high jumped, ran the mile relay. I think the first two years of high school, I was a lot better in track than in basketball. I watched a lot of track on TV. I always imagined myself being an Olympic star in track."

As a freshman at Shelby High School, Charlotte won a state championship in track. Yet as she moved through high school, she switched her allegiance to basketball. "Basketball was my first love. That's what I started out doing."

The second element that could have prevented her from playing major college basketball was her grades. "At first, I focused too much on basketball," she says. "That's all I wanted to do. I would come home after school and go to the playground and play basketball. But once I realized, *Hey, if I'm going to make it on the collegiate level, I have to have the grades to get there,* I did a turnaround." Charlotte improved her situation from "grades that weren't going to get me in college" to the B honor roll. "It was kind of scary thinking that I was able to get a scholarship to a Division I school but I might not be able to get in because of grades."

Once she turned that around, there was one more obstacle. Nobody knew about her. Well, she did receive All-State honors, was MVP of the team each year, and even was named a Kodak All-American honorable mention. But her team was not good enough to attract anyone's attention. College coaches often look for players who are not only good but who also come from a winning program.

"We never went outside our sectionals," Charlotte explains. "A lot of people didn't even know about me."

But for a person who readily acknowledges and recognizes God's will, it was no mystery that she was noticed by the brother of North Carolina women's basketball coach, Sylvia Hatchell. "I was fortunate to be discovered by him when he watched one of our games. That's how I was recruited by a Division I school when a lot of people didn't know about me."

Besides North Carolina, only Clemson showed interest in this future college All-American. Not even North Carolina State, where her famous uncle had turned the program around twenty years earlier, looked her way.

But, of course, as with game-winning three-pointers, you only need one—and Charlotte needed only one school to give her a chance to shine.

Besides the Big Shot in 1994, Smith had one other remarkable, newsworthy accomplishment at North Carolina. It happened during her senior year in Chapel Hill.

The Tar Heels were playing host to North Carolina A & T in a December game as they began to get set for the upcoming ACC season. Before many in the crowd who had come to Carmichael Auditorium that day were settled in their seats, Smith did something no one had done in ten years in women's college basketball.

The Aggies had taken the opening tip and were beginning to set up their offense when Charlotte stepped in and stole a pass from A & T's Samara Dobbins. She raced down court with the ball, leaped into the air, and slammed the ball through the basket.

Not since Georgeann Wells had dunked twice during the 1984–85 season while playing for West Virginia had a woman dunked in an NCAA game. This was nothing new to Charlotte. "I was dunking in high school," she says.

Move ahead a few years to Charlotte's first year with the ABL Colorado Xplosion. Would she be able to "xplode" to the basket and throw one down? Would she be the one to make this historic first in the ABL?

She tried. During the 1996–97 season, she went up for a tip-in, grabbed the ball, and tried to shove it down. But it hit the rim and bounded harmlessly and embarrassingly away.

Although Charlotte didn't get that first pro dunk in her first year, she did have a successful year.

But the season didn't start out well. In addition to dealing with the death of her mom, Charlotte had to battle some nagging injuries. First a hamstring injury. Then a twisted ankle.

After thirteen games, the team was 4-9. But then the team went on a tear. Led by leading scorer Crystal Robinson and by a healthy Charlotte Smith, the Xplosion won nineteen of its last twenty-three games to win the Western Conference.

Characteristic of Smith's improvement as the season wore on was her being named ABL Player of the Week in early February. On the basis of two exceptional performances in the final week of the season as the Xplosion clinched the Western Conference title, Smith was conferred the honor. She became the fourth Xplosion player to capture the award during the season.

Despite her successes with the Xplosion, Smith was shocked to find herself on the trading block after the season. After helping her team to a conference title and after being the number two scorer and rebounder on the team, and after getting a vote for league MVP, she was surprised to be considered expendable.

"When my general manager traded me, I was devastated," Smith recalls. "It was hard to understand."

Smith's agent spoke with league officials about her displeasure with being traded to the Seattle Reign, so a deal was worked out that sent her to the San Jose Lasers instead. That's where Smith began her second season in the ABL.

As she considers the trade and the subsequent events, Charlotte Smith comes back again to the philosophy that has guided her through the tough times as well as the good. It's a philosophy we all need. "Here it is again: Not my will, Lord, but Yours. I don't understand what is happening, but I know that everything happens for a reason to those who love God."

It's the kind of thinking that can make life always seem fresh and bright and new.

Q & A WITH CHARLOTTE SMITH

Q: *At North Carolina, you had a program to help you with jumping. What were some components of that program?*
Charlotte Smith: The program helped me increase my vertical leap and get more consistency in my dunking. We worked on explosive power in the weight room. We did squats, snatch squats, and leg presses with weights. We also did a lot of jumping on different size boxes.

Q: *What are some things you do to build yourself up spiritually?*
Charlotte: I like to listen to gospel music, like Yolanda Adams. Also, I like to listen to tapes from church services at the church I go to.

Q: *As a pioneer in women's pro basketball, what do you think is happening in girls' and women's basketball?*

Charlotte: Women's basketball is on the rise. You can see a lot of development in the early ages. The basketball camps, like the Nike All-American camp, are starting to groom women's basketball players earlier. They're learning the fundamentals earlier. Women are a lot more athletic than they were in the past. There are a lot of women who can dunk the ball. It's not out there yet. The game is a lot more fast-paced, a lot more athletic. There's been a lot more invested at an early age. They are starting out weight-training at an earlier age. Who knows, in the future, the women might be playing the game above the rim, which will take the game to another level.

Q: *When you speak at camps, do you have a chance to share your faith?*

Charlotte: I usually do a lot of speaking during the summer. I have the opportunity to speak at a lot of Nike camps. I talk about different life situations and how I dealt with them. I tell the campers that if you keep God first, and know that you can do all things through Him, you don't have to worry about the obstacles that come your way. Just keep the faith and stay positive. Everything will work out in God's way for those who love the Lord.

Rosalynn Sumners

World Champion Figure Skater
BACK WHERE SHE BELONGS

VITAL STATISTICS

Born: April 20, 1964, in Palo Alto, California
Height: 5′3″
Single
Residence: Edmonds, Washington
Special Interests: Reading Christian books

CAREER HONORS

1979: US Novice Champion
1980: World Junior Champion
1981: National Sports Festival Champion
1982: US Olympic Festival Champion
1982, 1983, 1984: US National Champion
1984: Olympic Silver Medalist
1991: Pro US Open Champion

OTHER HIGHLIGHTS

One of the original Stars on Ice
1995: Legends Championship, second place
1996: Legends Championship, third place
1996: Named Professional Skater of the Year

WARMING UP

Rosalynn Sumners has a special place in her heart for the people of war-scarred Sarajevo. It was in that once-beautiful city that she experienced her only Olympic moment in 1984. "We did a tribute to Sarajevo in Stars on Ice," she says of the skating extravaganza with which she has been associated for ten years. "It was done by Kitty and Peter Carruthers, Scott Hamilton, Brian Orser, and me. It was a pretty emotional event each night. Sometimes I see pictures from there—like the rink where we skated. It was turned into a morgue. Wood from the bleachers were made into coffins. It's really sad."

FAVORITE BIBLE PASSAGE

Take my yoke upon you and learn from me, for I am gentle and humble in heart, and you will find rest for your souls (Matthew 11:29).

Rosalynn Sumners

osalynn Sumners is grace on ice. Her fluid, majestic style carries her across the frozen surface like few other skaters. For the nearly two decades since she swept onto the national skating scene in 1979 as the US Novice Champion, millions of people have gazed in awe at the way she glides so effortlessly and punctuates her choreography with such class and beauty.

In the annals of US figure skating, Rosalynn's name will forever be mentioned along with other greats like Dorothy Hamill and Peggy Fleming. New, young talent will come along—some possessing more powerful triple jumps or more athletic double Axels. But rare will be the skater who can match Sumners in sheer artistic excellence.

Yet for all that grace and all that beauty and all that majesty, there will always be attached to Rosalynn's name one disturbing Fact. It's a Fact that seems unfair. So overplayed. So inconsequential in the big picture.

A televised skating competition that aired in the fall of 1997 is typical of how this Fact seems always to resurface when Rosalynn skates. In this TV event, as Sumners skated another of her beautiful routines to appropriate background music that guided her choreography, the commentators couldn't resist bringing up the Fact. It's not as if the viewers, presumably skating fans, didn't know the Fact already. Or as if after thirteen years the Fact needed to be hauled out again for public consumption.

The truth is, however, the Fact is inescapable. It is what ate at Rosalynn for years. It is what drove her to near perfection on the professional circuit. It's what changed her view toward her faith for a large portion of her adult life.

So what is this larger-than-life Fact that made such an impact on a young woman's life?

In 1984, Rosalynn Sumners, the reigning US and World Champion skater and a young woman of nineteen years who had driven herself relentlessly toward a single goal, skated her heart out on the world's stage at the 1984 Olympics in Sarajevo only to lose the gold medal to a woman from East Germany named Katarina Witt. Not only was that medal lost to Witt, it was lost by the narrowest of margins—one-tenth of a point. And to make matters even more painful, the judge whose low score spelled the difference was from neighboring Canada.

In the late Cold War years of the early 1980s, when the US and any country from the Communist bloc were considered mortal enemies, for a non-Communist, Western Hemisphere judge to allow that to happen was unthinkable.

A silver medal that for most skaters would have been a lifetime achievement for Rosalynn stood for defeat.

"I was completely devastated," she says. "That gold medal was what I had worked for the whole time. I felt like I had let everybody down. My city, Seattle, my parents, my family, my coach. Everyone who had put so much into me for all those years."

The irony of her feelings back then are not lost on Rosalynn. She refers to her friends and Stars on Ice partners Kitty and Peter Carruthers as an illustration. "They ended up winning the silver medal while I lost the gold medal. They weren't expected to do anything against the Russians. I was expected to win." Their silver was a triumph; hers seemed, to Rosalynn at least, a tragedy.

It is difficult for most people to understand what it must mean for an athlete to have the weight of great expectations riding on her shoulders. Yet it may help to understand the scope of those expectations to note that when *Sports Illustrated* put together its Winter Olympics Preview in February 1984, there on the cover under the heading "America's Best Bets" is Rosalynn Sumners, flanked by Scott Hamilton, Tamara McKinney, and Phil Mahre.

Pretty heady stuff for a teenager.

Going into the competition, Sumners knew she was under intense scrutiny. "I had won the World Championship in Helsinki in 1983 and was reigning world champion, so I was going into the Olympics as the favorite to win. It was a bit of an unusual position for me. I'd much rather be the underdog. I don't like having a lot of that kind of pressure on me. I'm much better under no pressure or just my own pressure. Going into the Olympics that year was not my favorite year I had ever gone through. There was so much pressure, so many expectations. As hard as my family and everyone tried not to make me feel it, it was there."

In the competition for the gold in women's free skating, Katarina had come out of the preliminary rounds with the lead, followed closely by Rosalynn. The first lady on the ice was Witt, who was superb. She showed both power and grace as she nailed three triple jumps in her routine. Her scores left little room for Rosalynn to surpass her. The Seattle native would have to be almost perfect to catch the woman from East Germany.

Sumners's program was nearly flawless as well, full of the beauty for which her routines were noted. However, when it came to the breathtaking power moves that she needed, she backed down just a bit. In her last two jumps, instead of going for broke, Rosalynn performed a double toe loop instead of a triple and a single instead of a double Axel. "I could have won if I had landed those jumps," she remarked after the competition.

It would be Sumners's one and only shot at Olympic gold. "Back then, it wasn't really known for skaters to go past age twenty in international competition," she says. "I talked it over with my parents and my coach, but I knew I wouldn't be back in 1988. I didn't have the personality that said, 'I've got to stay in.' I didn't have the energy or the desire to put in four more years. Besides, at age nineteen, I wanted a life. I wanted to date. I was tired of living that unbelievably sheltered lifestyle. It was time to grow up."

Up to that point in her life, growing up for Rosalynn had meant only one thing: Skating. Since she first stepped into a pair of skates on a Sunday afternoon in Edmonds, Washington, when she was seven years old, she seemed to be on a one-way trip to skating stardom.

That initial ice time was innocent enough. "When I was seven, my mom clipped a coupon out of the newspaper for a free public skate. We laugh about it because it was probably the last free thing in this sport." Rosalynn, along with some friends, went to the rink, and she was hooked.

"At first, all I wanted to do was to make my blade glide," she says. "I asked my mom for lessons so I could do that. I zipped through the lessons and went, 'OK, now what? That can't be it.' "

When Rosalynn's parents saw that their little girl needed more training than public lessons could provide, they hired Lorraine Borman as her private coach. Lorraine and Rosalynn would be together for the next twelve years—and beyond. Today, Rosalynn says of her, "She's more of a best friend than a coach."

As Rosalynn worked her way up through the local skating ranks and into national and international competition, having Borman close by was a distinct advantage. "I never had to leave home to train," she says. "I was a homebody. I was close to my family."

Rosalynn is quick to credit Borman with much of her success. "My personality is because of her. I almost spent more time with her than with my mom. She was very tough, but she did it in a way that made me not rebel. I never wanted to say, 'Excuse me, who are you to scream and yell and chase me around the ice?'

"I pushed her to push me. I would put notes under her door that would say, 'Work me harder.' "

Still today, Lorraine's instructions are bearing fruit. "I'll do something still—if I'm practicing and I make a mistake. I will not get off the ice until I do that right five times in a row. Here I am in my thirties doing the same things I did when I was ten.

"She wanted grace and beauty. I've lasted as long as I have because of the grace and beauty. Jumps were never natural with me. She put more focus on the artistic side."

For Rosalynn to get the training from her coach that she needed during her schooling years, some adjustments had to be made.

"I kept a normal schooling schedule through eighth grade, although my mother had to really fight with the school board. Tutoring [home schooling] was illegal in Washington at the time, but I had to do something to get the ice time I needed. So the school allowed me to skip such classes as home economics and physical education, and I was given credits for skating. I went to the main four classes, but I was the oddball of the school."

That didn't matter to Rosalynn, though. What mattered was skating.

During her high school years, there were further deviations from the norm. "I went to high school through an alternative education program set up for dropouts and pregnant girls. I would go in once a week, meet with the teachers, grab all my work, and go."

Rosalynn contends that she didn't miss "normal" high school life. "I went to one-half of a football game in high school once with a friend, and I just sat there like, 'This is so stupid.' I didn't get it. I thought it was so boring and such a waste of time.

"All I wanted to do was be a champion. I didn't care what it took. I had no desire to go to college. I never had that whole school desire. I loved school. I was a straight A student—the harder the teachers, the more I like them—but I was never into that extracurricular stuff."

It was a drive that is almost unexplainable. Trying to explain it, Rosalynn says, "Nobody knows where it came from. My mom played violin and her dad was a conductor. The minute he pushed her to be competitive, she put it down. My dad was a math major, not much of an athlete. Obviously, God gave me the drive to excel."

If her parents didn't give her the inborn drive, they at least gave Rosalynn the opportunity. "I had parents who completely supported me. It was ridiculously expensive. I couldn't make money at what I was doing because I was an amateur. More than once, they said, 'Hey, if you want to give this up, we are more than willing to support you.' My mom always said that her responsibility was that if a parent has a kid who shows talent, the parent's responsibility is to give that child everything to accomplish that."

So, with Lorraine Borman's teaching, her own relentless drive, and her parents' support, Rosalynn was on her way as a skater. She won every event she entered on the local level and was soon competing nationally.

When she was fifteen, Rosalynn became the US Novice Champion, and the next year she captured the World Junior title.

As a Junior, though, she was not yet eligible to compete in the Olympics.

Beginning in 1982, she began a three-year run as the US National Champion.

And then there was the 1983 World Champion title she won in Helsinki.

Everything was in order. She was right on track with the four-year game plan that she and Lorraine had put together, culminating in the big prize—the gold medal in Sarajevo. When it didn't come, with younger skaters like Elaine Zayak and Tiffany Chin coming up behind her, Rosalynn gave up on the gold.

A quest for Olympic gold was not the only thing Rosalynn gave up after her silver at Sarajevo. She also abandoned her walk with the Lord. Her anger and frustration over the second-place finish spilled over into her spiritual life.

"I grew up as a Christian," she says. "I have journals that I kept leading up to the Olympics in which I wrote down my prayers. One of my favorite books was *Peace and Love*, the story of skater Janet Lynn, who is a Christian."

Yet that disappointment in Yugoslavia was so all-encompassing that Rosalynn let it affect her relationship with God. Maybe she had never been discipled properly, or perhaps she was just too young spiritually to understand how God works, but Rosalynn allowed a faulty view of God to color her relationship with Him. "After I didn't win the Olympics, I was like, 'I'm out of here. Thanks a lot, God. You led me all the way up to the national champion, world championships, right up to the last second of the Olympics, and I don't win.'

"In my 19-year-old mind, it was sort of like, 'Thanks, You let me down.' So I made this weird decision. I decided to sort of do it on my own. I thought, *You're no help; I'll do it on my own.*" Weird indeed, for it would rob her of more than a decade of fellowship with God.

For the next eleven years, Rosalynn took her skating show on the road as a professional. For a couple of years, she toured with Disney on Ice. "I really struggled with that. It was fourteen shows a week, and I was sitting in the same city for two weeks at a time."

Much has changed in skating, though, since Rosalynn's early days on the professional circuit. For one thing, the sport of skating has become much more popular than it was then. "Now, each event is either prime time or huge money, not that the money is the most important thing. It's a much bigger, much more exciting sport than it was twelve years ago."

Another thing that has changed is the addition of Discover Stars on Ice, which Sumners has been a part of since it began. "On the Stars on Ice tour, because it is a different city every night, it's a whole new peg of energy. We have such an amazing group of talents, such an amazing talent, that there's no chance to let down your motivation. Because I'm a little closer to the end of my career, there isn't a night I don't go out there and relish every second."

Night after night the Discover Stars on Ice perform before capacity crowds in the nation's largest arenas. For a skater who grew up learning to skate for the judges, it was a bit of a change for Rosalynn to learn to skate for the crowd.

"I don't necessarily really live for the crowd. I actually had to learn how to be a performer, whereas someone like Scott Hamilton was a born performer. It is natural for him to perform. I am more of a technical skater. It took me a little longer to be a performer and to understand the expectations of the audience.

"I just skated because Rosalynn wanted to skate. It wasn't so that I could entertain people necessarily. I loved being out there, but I didn't quite get it that I should entertain the crowd. Now I try to move the audience; I use them a little as my motivation, but my motivation comes from within me. And I'm harder on myself, putting pressure on myself, wondering, *OK, what is the audience going to think tonight?* I try to pick music that will entertain, but it's not what I live for."

For most of Rosalynn's professional career, she lived for herself. Still suffering from her feelings of despair over that Olympic experience, she lived the next eleven years without a day-to-day relationship with God.

"I had people here and there mentioning stuff about faith. For instance, I had a manager who was a Christian. In fact, the Bible I now use was one he had given me for Christmas in 1983.

"But as I went through my career, I didn't think I needed to depend on Christ. Looking back, I know that's a joke, because I was very unhappy.

"I was unhappy the first couple of years on Disney.

"Then I slowly started building my self-esteem back up. I really built a strong reputation as a professional. I was never out of work. As the work got bigger, I was sort of going along with it.

"However, as my pro career was going one direction, my personal life was going another. I had some of what I would call self-destructive behavior. Nothing that people would consider major or serious like drugs or alcohol, just some things that were just not great."

In 1995, though, something happened that brought Rosalynn back to her spiritual roots.

The Discover Stars on Ice production manager, Steven Schwirtz, was a Christian, and had been with the crew since 1990. During a visit by the Stars on Ice show to Seattle, Rosalynn asked Steven to have dinner at her house.

"When he came to my house, he had a CD with him. He put it in the player, and we listened to it. It was sort of rock and roll. He showed me the front of the CD, and it said, 'Stryper.'

"I looked at it and said, 'Stryper, Stryper. Why do I know that name?'

"He said, 'It was a Christian rock band in the '80s.'

"Then I pointed to something else on the cover and said, 'What is that?'

"He said, 'It's a verse.'

"I said, 'I know it's a Bible verse, but what does the verse say?'

"He told me, 'It says, "By His stripes we are healed."'

"It was the weirdest thing. As soon he said those words, we both just looked at each other and started to bawl. I just started to cry. I didn't even know he was a Christian. He was not what you would think a Christian would look like. He had long hair, and he had been in a Christian rock and roll band as a teenager. You wouldn't even know he was a Christian.

"Right then and there, I totally rededicated my life to the Lord. All of a sudden I said, 'What was I doing for ten years?'" She realized how wrong she had been to put her relationship with Christ on hold because of a disappointing ice skating event. Since that spring day in 1995, Sumners has been, as she describes it, "gung ho" about her faith in Christ.

For Rosalynn, besides the Scriptures and church, growth in her faith depends on friends, books, and prayer.

As for friends, she found "a wonderful church in Seattle." When she has to be gone, friends send her tapes of the services. While on the road, she and fellow Christian Paul Wylie pray before every show and "have a bit of Bible study" whenever possible.

Another friend she and Paul have recently struck up a relationship with is Michael W. Smith. Paul knew Michael and asked Rosalynn to join him to have lunch with the singer.

But then Paul called Rosalynn and told her, "We can't have lunch with Michael, but we are going on his private plane to Tupelo, Mississippi, to a Franklin Graham crusade." Which is what they did.

"Through that whole thing, Michael's people wanted to connect the singing and the skating, so we've begun talking about doing some projects together. We could do an unbelievable video with music and skating and do it for some sort of Christian charity."

As for books, Rosalynn says, "I love to gobble up books. I go toward books that guide you to the Bible—that help me know where to turn in the Bible."

As for prayer, Roz says, "I could do twenty-four hours of prayer." Combining the two, she says one of the best books she has read is *Prayer, The Great Adventure*.

Rosalynn Sumners's life has been a great adventure as well. After a remarkable amateur career and a successful decade-plus as a professional, she appears ready for a new phase of life. As she contemplates moving away from the Stars on Ice Tour and into other things, she says, "I don't want to quit cold turkey. It is my life. When the Stars is gone, it will be sad."

But she will keep skating. Keep dazzling the crowd with her grace. And perhaps there's another thing she would like to do. "I'd like to speak. I'd like to tell people about an athlete who set a goal, came short, felt that God let me down, lived a life on the road that looks glamorous, and how God never left me. He was there when I needed Him."

That's a story worth listening to.

Q & A WITH ROSALYNN SUMNERS

Q: *What would you say was the highlight of your career?*
Rosalynn Sumners: I think it was my first US title. I was seventeen, and Elaine Zayak had already been crowned champion. She was crowned the national champion right after the 1980 Olympics. Back then, it was rare to dethrone a champion. This was sort of a political, unspoken thing in the United States Figure Skating Association. What they wanted was to send a four-time national champion to the Olympics, which looked stronger and was a little more political.

In the year leading up to that, I had been skating well, and my only goal in life was to win the national championship. A week before the championships, I pulled a muscle in my hip, which, as it turns out, was really the only injury I have ever had.

I went in very frustrated. My goal looked like it was not going to be too easy. Every top girl that night skated awful. Elaine fell four times in her program, and I was the last competitor to do one triple. I kind of ad-libbed with a bunch of double Axels, and I won.

That's sort of what changed that part of the sport. Now it's like whoever skates best can win now. I changed that. I was the first one to dethrone a champion in a long time. It was unexpected because I was injured. That night of all of them was the most special.

Q: *What changed when you rededicated your life to Christ?*
Rosalynn: Part of everything becomes easier, and other things become harder. You make mistakes, or you do what you know is wrong or you trust the wrong things in your life, and you know you're not putting your faith in the right place. You get bombarded a lot from the outside world. People don't like you to talk about your faith. But you have an inner strength, and Someone to turn to. Now there's a much bigger picture. Now I can say, "OK, God, I don't know why this is happening, but it's all in Your hands."

Sheila Taormina

1996 Olympic Gold Medalist: Swimming
GIVING TILL IT HURTS

VITAL STATISTICS

Born: March 18, 1969, in Detroit, Michigan
Height: 5'3"
College: University of Georgia; also MBA from Georgia
Single
Residence: Livonia, Michigan
Special Interests: Speaking, visiting family members

CAREER HONORS

1996: Olympic gold medal, 4 x 200 freestyle relay
National champion
State swimming champion, senior year of high school

OTHER HIGHLIGHTS

1987: Olympic Festival, 400m IM bronze medal
1991: World University Games, 400-meter IM silver medal
1995: US Open 200-meter freestyle champion
Sixth in 200-meter freestyle at 1996 Olympic trials

WARMING UP

Before the 1996 Olympics, Sheila Taormina and her family of seven brothers and sisters had not been together for eight years. So, when the folks at the Olympic committee asked her how many tickets she wanted for the day she was going to swim in Atlanta, she said, "I'll need twenty-five." The response of the committee representative was disbelief. "You know, Sheila, other people are swimming that day too," Taormina was told. However, when the committee members did their tallying, they discovered that indeed they had an allotment of twenty-five for the Taormina family. That only created a new problem. "That'll be $4,000," Sheila was told. So Sheila and her family decided to raise the money. One of her sisters, an artist, designed a T-shirt that promoted World Friendship. Through word of mouth and churches that sold them, the family raised the money for everyone to go to Atlanta for the Great Taormina Reunion.

FAVORITE BIBLE PASSAGE

Do not store up for yourselves treasures on earth, where moth and rust destroy, and where thieves break in and steal. But store up for yourselves treasures in heaven. . . . For where your treasure is, there your heart will be also (Matthew 6:19–21).

"That's by far my favorite," Sheila says. "I'm the kind of person who likes nice things. I want a nice car and a house and a Jacuzzi. I need to be reminded that those things aren't going to last. Those things can't buy eternal life."

Sheila Taormina

Sheila Taormina, whose home in Livonia, Michigan, is not far from the home of the Detroit Red Wings, treats her hard-earned prized possession much like the Red Wings handled their Stanley Cup.

The Cup is one of the most coveted trophies in sports. Yet the Red Wings Cup was not handled as though it were some fragile piece of fine china. It is passed around, used as a drinking chalice, dropped, and in many ways mishandled.

What Sheila owns is also a much-sought-after prize—perhaps the single-most desired award in all of sports. She has a gold medal from the 1996 Olympic Games. But she isn't shy about letting others enjoy it.

What she went through to earn that medal is worth describing.

When she was just a little kid, she and her twin brother Steven—the last of the Taorminas' eight children—grew tired of waiting for an older sister who was being taken to swimming lessons. So they asked their mom if they could take lessons too. She signed them up, and they dove into a new sport.

The twins stuck with swimming all the way through high school. Sheila also participated in track in school, but swimming took precedence. At Livonia Stephenson High School, that was not unusual, because the school was noted for its swimming program.

When Sheila was a senior, she captured the state title in every event.

This year of triumph was 1987. She still had to train nine more years before that victorious summer evening in the pool at Atlanta. In between, she carved out a successful record in swimming at the University of Georgia, went to three Olympic trials, captured medals at the World University Games and the Olympic festival, and earned an undergraduate degree in business and a masters in business administration at Georgia.

By the time she held that gold medal in her hand, Sheila Taormina had surely earned the right to cherish it. To admire it. To hide it away. To fear for its safety. To value it as a lifelong achievement. To turn it into a mountain of money as so many others have done.

But to think that she might do that would be to ignore an important life reality that had occurred a year before she jumped into the Olympic waters and came out a world champion. Thinking that the Olympic medal would turn Sheila into anything less than a champion underestimates the kind of woman she was.

Let's go back to her final year of high school as she was beginning to decide what college would win her attention and benefit from her swimming skills. The most logical choice, it seems, would be for Sheila to travel just a few miles south and west of Livonia and enter the University of Michigan. The Wolverines boasted a strong swimming program under the coaching of Jim Richardson, and the proximity would make it easy for the family to come watch her swim for the Maize and Blue.

But one thing held Sheila back. She had read in a swimming magazine that Richardson was something of an outspoken Christian, and she didn't want anything to do with that. Although she was a churchgoer at her mother's request, Sheila didn't especially enjoy the experience. "Mostly, I would look at my watch and daydream," she says of her church experience. "I didn't want to go to a school where the coach was going to pray before practice."

So she made her decision to go to the University of Georgia, where she really liked what she saw of the coaching staff. It may have been the right move for her athletically, but if she wanted to steer clear of Christians, she had made a huge tactical error.

"I landed right in the heart of the Bible belt," she says now.

The first inkling she had that she hadn't escaped God's attention by fleeing south was when she met a couple of guys in her dorm. David and Ashley lived across the hall, and as soon as she moved in, they began inviting her to Bible studies they held on Sunday night.

"This was my first encounter with someone who was a Christian and made it a big part of his life," she says. "It actually scared me at first." The more the young men asked her to attend the Bible study, the more excuses Sheila came up with.

Finally, though, they got her to go. "I was totally lost. I didn't know the difference between the Old and New Testaments. I couldn't answer any of the questions in the Bible study. I didn't know anything about the Bible. I had never heard that Jesus died on the cross. But when I heard it, I was interested. I thought, 'Wow, you mean He did that for us?' "

Later, a member of the swim team at Georgia asked Sheila to attend church with her. "It was one of those stand up and clap churches. I was uncomfortable, but I loved it. They had enthusiasm. They had life. These people were having the time of their lives."

This time, Sheila did not look at her watch and daydream. She began to consider what was being said.

Another important part of Sheila's spiritual journey took place in 1991 when she went to England to compete in the World University Games. Because she was scheduled to swim on the first day of the Games, she didn't attend the opening ceremonies. Instead, she and some teammates went by invitation to a chapel, where a TV was supposed to be on so they could watch the ceremonies. However, the TV didn't work, and Sheila and the other visitors were left to chat with a chaplain who had opened the chapel.

"I thought, *Oh, no, we're stuck with this guy. He's going to talk to us about religion.* But he was really neat. He had some tea and cookies for us, and we talked about a lot of different subjects. At the end, he gave us each a New Testament and wrote in it, 'As a souvenir of the World University Games.' "

This simple gift would be very important in Sheila's life. Two years later, she found it while unpacking some boxes. Inside the Testament was a reading schedule, promising to get her through the Bible in two years. Sheila took up the challenge and read faithfully until she had read the whole thing.

Despite all of these influences, Sheila was still not a Christian. "For six years, it was a piece here, a piece there. I needed a lot of people talking to me. A lot of study."

Finally, in September 1995, Sheila made an appointment to talk with the pastor of New Focus Community Church near her home in Livonia. As Pastor Phil Rogers talked with her, he asked her specifically if she was a Christian. When Sheila said she wasn't sure, Rogers spelled out the gospel in simple terms. Finally, after several years of heading toward this moment, Sheila prayed to trust Jesus as her Savior.

Still ahead on the horizon for Taormina were the 1996 Olympic Games in Atlanta. Sheila was twenty-seven years old when the American trials rolled around, and she knew this would probably be her last shot at the gold. Perhaps she would experience less stress this year, since she had been in the trials two times before.

Not so, Sheila says. "The 1996 trials were stressful because I knew I might make the team. Before, I knew I wouldn't make it."

Sheila's coach, Craig Phill, who had been working with her since she was nine, must have sensed the stress. "He sat down with me a week before the Olympic trials, and he told me that I had already succeeded. Whether I made the team or not, I had already succeeded. The most important thing to him was his wife and his two kids, and the way I swam was not what mattered to him. I had trained really hard. And he said that I had succeeded already because of the preparation."

With that kind of mind-set, Sheila went to the trials and made the twenty-member US women's swim team. By finishing sixth in the 200-meter freestyle event at the trials, she won a spot on the team that would be competing in Atlanta.

On Thursday, July 25, 1996, Sheila got her chance to swim for gold as a member of the four-member 4 x 200 team. Earning a spot on that squad was a complicated endeavor. First, she had to qualify for the finals by virtue of her performance in a preliminary round earlier in the Olympics. In that round, the American women who had recorded the third through sixth fastest times at the trials were put together to swim the 4 x 200.

On the sidelines as those women swam, waiting their turn to swim in the finals, were Trina Jackson and Cristina Teuscher. They had finished first and second in the trials and were already assured that they would be swimming in the finals. Also watching was Jenny Thompson. Thompson, who had not qualified for this event because she finished seventh in the trials, had qualified in another event and was a part of the twenty-member US team. Despite her failure to get a Top Six score at the trials, the coaches knew she could help the team. For instance, a month before the Olympics, she swam a 200-meter freestyle in a time that would have put her third at the qualifiers. Therefore, the coaches wanted her to be a part of the finals 4 x 200 team along with Teuscher and Jackson. With Teuscher, Jackson, and Thompson possessing three spots of the relay team for the finals, there would be just one spot open. Therefore, in the preliminary, four women were swimming for that single slot—unless they could beat Thompson's time from a month earlier.

It could be every woman for herself—or it could be a team effort. The US preliminary squad decided to go for the team approach. "All four of us decided that morning that we were going to break the US record," Sheila says. "We set a team goal. We had to do that so we wouldn't look at each other as competitors. We didn't break the US record, but we ended up walking away happy. We placed the USA team in first place going into the finals."

An observer could imagine the pressure these women were under. But Sheila didn't think about it that way. "Some people don't do well under pressure," she says. "They are thinking so much about the outcome. *Will I be in the finals? Will we win the gold medal?* I had learned in my last two years of swimming that I was just blessed to be in this sport. No matter what came my way, as long as I was trying my hardest, that was what should make you smile when you walk away.

"I learned that through people. By myself I used to put pressure on myself. But once I started listening to people, I had such great support. My family couldn't care less if I was in the finals. They were just having such a great time when they were together. The people in my church didn't expect anything from me. They just said, 'Come back happy. Whether you have a gold medal or not.' "

So, unencumbered by pressure, Sheila led her preliminary team to a time that put the US team in first place going into the finals. And she clocked the fastest time, earning that last spot on the team that would be swimming for the gold.

Later that evening, Taormina, Thompson, Teuscher, and Jackson breezed past Germany and Australia to take the gold medal.

That gold medal changed so much for Taormina. But as she stood on the podium after receiving it, she decided immediately that she was going to use it for more than just self-promotion.

"I knew that now little kids would be watching me more, and I had more of an opportunity to influence young people. I remember standing on the awards stand and thinking, *OK, God, what am I supposed to do with this now?*

"I know it's not meant for me just to take it and give myself a pat on the back. So I was kind of burdened about what am I to do? How do I direct my life? You have all these good feelings, but you also have this weight of responsibility."

Right away, then, Sheila knew that this was not a safety-deposit-box kind of award. This was not something she could keep to herself. Just as the Stanley Cup is the people's trophy, this was the people's gold medal.

In an age of me-me-me athletes whose success often seems to make them have selective amnesia—they forget everyone else—it is exciting to know what Sheila did next. Although it was a learning time for her, and she made some mistakes over the next few months, it's a refreshing story nonetheless.

Armed with the knowledge that God gave her this medal as a tool, she opened her heart and life to everyone who wanted a piece of it.

"I came home and I didn't want to be perceived as an athlete who was stuck-up and wouldn't give back."

So whenever anyone called, Sheila said yes. She didn't charge for her services, and she didn't turn any request down. "I came back with the intention to go to whatever group wants me. I'll bend over backwards to get there and I'm not going to charge a penny. I thought I'd be busy for a month going to the schools and swim teams and doing some talks and motivating swimmers."

Three months later, things had not let up. Request after

request came in, and Sheila kept going out to make appearances. "It was insane," she says. "Every weekend I was flying somewhere. Almost every weeknight I was driving to talk to some group, and I also had a full-time job. I ended up missing my church every Sunday. I ended up not having any personal time. I started having anxiety attacks. I was having trouble sleeping at night. I was worried I might miss an appointment or I might not have the directions to the next event." The woman who had learned to withstand the pressure of going for the gold was succumbing to the pressure of good intentions.

Sheila tells a story that illustrates the problem she had created by her accessibility. "One guy from a nearby city called and asked, 'Can you come to our parade on the Fourth of July?'

"I told him I was supposed to be in Providence, Rhode Island, that weekend at a swim camp. So he asked, 'On the Fourth itself are you coaching?'

"When I said no, he said, 'Why don't you fly back on Friday night after you're done, do the parade on Saturday, and fly back to Rhode Island?'

"I said, 'Well, that's a lot of travel.'

"He couldn't pay my plane fare. He wanted me to use my frequent flyer miles. The amazing thing is, I actually considered doing it. Then I slapped myself in the face and said to myself, 'What are you doing?' "

Finally, physically and mentally exhausted, she began to ask advice of people she trusted. They told her it was OK to say no to people. That it was all right to charge for her services. That if she took care of everyone else and not herself, she would end up hurting everyone. "I finally learned that you're not a bad person for not being able to help everyone out. Good people were telling me, 'You're not bad if you say no.' "

More than a year after coming home from Atlanta, Sheila was still in demand. "When you talk to one group, they talk to the next. I've flown all over the country and even out of the country."

She quit her job and concentrated on being Sheila Taormina, gold medal winner. She discovered that people were more than willing to pay a fee for her work, and she found out that those she told no were not at all upset with her.

Wherever she goes on the Sheila Taormina Goodwill Tour, Sheila takes with her a couple of things she didn't have a few years ago. First, she takes with her the knowledge that God has a plan for her life and a purpose for her fame. She knows that one of the key things she is supposed to teach people who come to hear her is that the value in a person's life is not whether he or she becomes a big star. "A lot of people are getting the message that the people we value are the Michael Jordans and the Shaquille O'Neals. I want kids to know that their value is not there. It is in their value in God's eyes."

The second truth Sheila wants to teach comes out in the way she allows her gold medal to be treated. "I go out and speak, and I let people pass around the medal. Sometimes I lose track of where it is in the crowd. People say, 'How can you pass that around?'

"It's been dropped and dinged up. The ribbon has been dragged through a hot fudge sundae by a little boy at a restaurant. It just doesn't bother me. That's not going to buy you eternal life. We need to teach kids about the gold medal that will last forever."

Q & A WITH SHEILA TAORMINA

Q: *How did your parents guide you in your swimming career?*
Sheila Taormina: All the years I swam, my parents never wanted me to feel like I was swimming for them. One time I called them from college during my sophomore year because I was so homesick I wanted to quit swimming. They just said, "We want you to be happy. We don't care about the full scholarship. If you want to come home, we'll pay for your college here." They were amazing that way. A lot of parents put too much pressure on their kids.

Q: *You must have learned a lot from your five older sisters. What is something valuable you got from them?*
Sheila: I'm fortunate to have five older sisters who kept telling me, "Girl, just keep getting faster as you keep getting older." You hear a lot of times that after you're eighteen, it's over. My sisters kept saying, "No way, you're just going to keep getting better." They helped me out by telling me that.

Q: *Do you think of yourself as a representative of women in sports?*
Sheila: I'm a representative of older women in sports. I think that women think once you get past college, after eighteen you're fat and slow. It's all downhill from there. But you can keep getting better and better. You have to change your eating habits. Stretch a little more. Battle some things. But you don't have to stop getting better.

Also, I like to remind women that you can do more than one thing at a time. You don't have to be just a student or just a mother; you can be a couple of things. You have the strength and energy to do that.

Q: *You were a young Christian at Atlanta in the 1996 Olympics. How did your faith help you at the time?*
Sheila: It helped me to know that your value doesn't lie in the place you get in the Olympics. You focus on what you have. My faith taught me not to expect anything. I just went in there saying, "I have so much. I'm so blessed already." For me to expect anything more, that's when the pressure comes in.

That's why we have a problem in athletics with steroids and performance-enhancing drugs. People think they have to be valuable—and so people who don't think they can do that with hard work use these other methods. These are people who don't understand that their value lies in how God views them.

My faith in the Lord helped me relax. No expectations, just thankfulness to Him.

Wendy Ward
Professional Golfer
VICTORY AT THE CROSSROADS

VITAL STATISTICS

Born: May 6, 1973, in San Antonio, Texas
Height: 5'9"
College: Graduated from Arizona State University
Residence: San Antonio, Texas
Special Interests: Bowling, playing the piano, Nate Hair
Turned Professional: 1995

1997: Fieldcrest Cannon Classic

1992: Texas State Women's champion
1993: NCAA championship: third place
1994: NCAA championship: runner-up
1994: US Women's Amateur champion
1994: World Team Amateur champion
1994: Member, US Curtis Cup team
1993–95: Team national championship, Arizona State
1993–95: First Team All-American
1995: NCAA championships: runner-up

As a professional golfer, Wendy Ward understands the importance of knowing the basics and putting them into practice. As a Christian, she has learned that the same lesson applies to practicing her faith. One way she helps keep the basics in front of her is with a small book that she has had since her college days at Arizona State. "It's kind of like a concordance," Wendy says. "It gives references for what the Bible says about certain things. For example, one of the biggest problems on the Tour is gossip, and that drives me nuts. So I look in the book and see where to look in the Bible to read about gossip. It helps me find God's prescription for how to deal with it."

"After I really got serious about my faith, the first verse I came across was in James 1:2–4. It says you're going to have trials and temptations and that God has a reason for them. Until He's finished preparing you and making you perfect, you have to keep persevering. When you've persevered, you'll receive a reward."

Wendy Ward

I t was Tuesday, September 23, 1997, two days before Wendy Ward would tee it up at the Fieldcrest Cannon Classic in Cornelius, North Carolina. Ward was about to wrap up her second full season on the Ladies Professional Golf Association (LPGA) Tour.

Wendy and a writer were discussing her career, which in the eyes of some observers had not quite lived up to the advance billing. After all, Ward had put together an amateur career that would have made Tiger Woods proud.

While a student-athlete at Arizona State University, Ward had won enough hardware to equip a trophy shop. She had captured the US Amateur title in 1992. Three times she had been named an All-American golfer at ASU. Twice she was runner-up for the NCAA championship.

So it was pretty much accepted that when she hit the pro circuit, she would find success just as easily.

But it hadn't happened. During Ward's first full year on the Tour in 1996, she had played in twenty-three events, but her highest finish in any of those tournaments was a tie for ninth, which she accomplished twice. For her efforts, Ward had finished seventy-fifth among the women on the Tour in winnings.

Her sophomore year on the LPGA circuit was going a little better. She had cranked her rankings up to sixty-fifth place going into the final tournament of the year. Her earnings were up, and she had finished in the Top 20 several times.

Yet she was hard-pressed to find an answer to what was holding her back. Ever enthusiastic and always positive, Ward was not letting her slow start on the Tour defeat her. Instead, as she sat in her hotel room in North Carolina and thought back over her short career, she felt she knew what was happening—and, true to her spirit, she was able to view things positively.

"I'm still learning about the Tour. This is the best of the best. The cream of the crop. There's no room for error.

"I look at my career as a mirror of my college career. Some of the golf courses I'm seeing only for the second time, and I feel like a freshman or maybe a sophomore. My career in college golf didn't really get off the ground until my junior year. I won one tournament as a sophomore at the end of the year, and that was more of a confidence boost. Then all of a sudden the next year I was able to take it and run with it."

Keep that fact in mind: end of sophomore year—one win.

"God alone knows the time frame. All I know is that He keeps telling me, 'This is the place I want you to be.' I do keep improving slowly but surely."

The pressures of living up to those high expectations based on a successful amateur career come from several sources.

One is the pressure to make a living. In a sport where you don't get paid if you don't do well, there is an intense pressure to succeed. "If we have a lousy weekend," Ward observes, "we could lose out. We still have a caddie to pay and our expenses. There are quite a lot of pressures."

Second is the self-imposed pressure that any good athlete puts on herself. "I have very high expectations for myself," she says. "I always have. That's where I have to step back and say, 'Whose expectations are we trying to fulfill here?'

"My high expectations are one of the big reasons I've been successful. I always feel that I need to achieve more and more, which is, I believe, the way God wants us to be. I don't think He wants us to be so content that we don't keep pressing forward.

"At the same time, I sit back and I say, 'God, where do You have me? Where do You want me to be? What are my needs? Am I fulfilling my needs and basic obligations?' I'm doing that.

"As far as my career is concerned, I've always moved in a positive direction. They say, 'Two steps forward, one step backward,' but I really feel that I'm gaining ground on the direction God has me going now. Would I have loved to have won a tournament by now or have had more Top 10 finishes? I would say, sure. I would be lying if I didn't. But at the same time, I am happy with where I am."

Pressure to pay the bills, pressure to fulfill internal and God-directed goals—Ward had been tackling those two problems well.

The third is harder to handle. Expectations from others.

"I've had a lot of people come up to me and say, 'We thought you would have performed better out here on tour.' One of the toughest battles out here is not the course or it's not the competitors, it's what everyone else wants to think and criticize." Those pressures had been eating at Wendy after two years on the Tour without a victory.

But on this day, as she talks with a writer about her career and reflects her thoughts about it, she reveals something important. Something vital to any athlete who succeeds.

"As I was driving home today from practice at the course where we'll play the Fieldcrest Cannon Classic, for some reason the thoughts of other people's expectations went across my mind. Immediately the Holy Spirit said to me, 'You know what, Wendy, if you listen to what they're saying, then you're putting your faith and trust in the human race. You're not putting your faith in Me and what I have planned for you.'

"It was like a fork in the road for me. A crossroads. It's funny that we're talking about this today. It kind of puts things back into perspective. It reminds me who I'm supposed to be serving."

With a renewed focus on whom she was playing golf for, Wendy Ward went to work on the Peninsula Club course. Keep in mind that in seventy-four competitive rounds of pro golf up until this week, Ward had broken 70 four times but she had not shot a round under 68.

But watch what happened.

On Thursday, she attacked the 6,318-yard course like it was a Putt-Putt course, shooting a 66. The next day she did even better, playing the course that lies hard by the shore of Lake Norman—home of many of Charlotte's richest athletes—in 65. Two days into the tournament, Ward had put together an incredible 131 over 36 holes.

But she wasn't done. On Saturday, she shot nearly eight strokes under her average for 1996, carding an unbelievable 64. She stood 21 strokes under par going into the final day's play.

On Sunday, she stroked birdies on the fourth and fifth holes and closed out with thirteen consecutive pars to finish with a two-under-par 70 for the day. When the dust cleared, Ward had done what no woman golfer had ever done on the LPGA Tour. She had finished an unbelievable 23 strokes under par, breaking the record of 20-under shared by Beth Daniel and Nancy Lopez.

And perhaps more important, she had won her first LPGA title.

Was it the crossroads decision she had made on Tuesday that spelled the difference? Or was it simply one good shot that led to another and another and another?

No one can say for sure. All Ward knew for certain was that despite being "a little frustrated with God's timing," she knew that He wanted her to "hang in there" and continue to do her best.

Her best became the best ever.

Wendy Ward had been aiming at this kind of day ever since she was a seven-year-old first-time hacker in Maryland where she lived with her sister Pam and their parents. John Ward was in the Army during the week and a recreational golfer on Saturday. In addition, the girls' mom was a two-or-three-days-a-week golfer, so it was natural for Pam and Wendy to take it up.

When Wendy was eleven, the family moved to San Antonio. It was there, when she was in middle school, that she first realized that she was a better-than-average golfer. "The high school coach came over to me and said to my dad, 'Would Wendy like to play with the high school team sometime?'

"I thought, *I'm not in high school.* At that point, a two-year age difference is huge. It was like, 'Wow! That person's a sophomore in high school!'

"But my dad said, 'Sure, we can line it up sometime.'"

Despite her initial misgivings about having to be thrust into the older group, Wendy soon discovered that age was not as much of a factor as ability. And she obviously had that.

"I realized when I played with those girls that there was only one out of the five or six who were there that presented me with a challenge as far as being able to beat me. I thought, *If this is what high school golf is like, I'm ready.*"

Wendy did quite well at that level, and her game began to get citywide exposure as she won some tournaments.

One of the obstacles she had to face in high school was that the coaches encouraged the athletes to play only one sport. They believed that an athlete who competed in two or three sports would be spread too thin and would not be as competitive.

"That was a tough decision for me to make, because it meant I wasn't going to go play one of the cooler sports. Also, none of my friends were going to go play golf." It was another of those forks in the road, and she obviously picked the correct route.

"As a junior, I started playing more nationally, and college coaches could come and see me play. There was a tour, the American Junior Golf Association, and just about every player coming up from college to the LPGA Tour has been on that tour."

Another obstacle presented itself in her senior year. By then, she was the only girl left to play golf at her high school. Therefore, she had to play on the guys' team.

It wasn't necessarily easier, but it worked out to her benefit. "I had to play from the blue tees when I played with the guys, which was all right. I didn't want to have to move to the ladies' tees. The boys didn't appreciate it on the few rounds when I beat them, but they accepted me OK.

"It was a learning experience. There was a lot I could learn from the guys that I wouldn't necessarily learn from the girls. I learned a lot about the basics: patience, course management. The guys could hit it a lot farther than I could, but if I just stayed within my own game, I could beat them any day of the week."

From high school in San Antonio, Wendy took her next big step toward golf stardom when she enrolled at Arizona State. "I wanted to stay in Texas," she says, "but there was something inside me that said I need to spread my wings and be on my own."

But there was something else. "Arizona State had a nice teaser for a golfer like me. They had just won the NCAA title, and I knew that if they won one, we could probably win it again."

For Ward, college life had a surprise package wrapped inside, a package she didn't even know she needed.

Growing up, Wendy had been a regular churchgoer. In fact, the whole family was at church every Sunday. "My parents sang in the choir. We went to Sunday school or when we were old enough they said we could either go to Sunday school or sit in the morning service. We decided to go to church because that was the more adult thing to do. Our family is musical and I enjoyed the singing. I would rather not sit in the classroom for an hour when I can sit in the sanctuary and sing some songs and get to listen and stand up and sit down. That was more fun."

Fun, but perhaps not eternally significant.

"We had that day at church, then we'd go live our life the rest of the week the way we wanted. There was a blessing at meals, but as far as prayer time or Bible study at home, that's just something that we didn't practice."

As a result, Wendy did not live a life that was dedicated to Jesus Christ. She had accepted Jesus as her Savior, but she didn't let Him make a difference in her life.

In fact, when she took off for Arizona State, she became a very negative person.

One person who noticed was Lori Brock, Wendy's golf pro. "She was a big part in getting me back into my walk with Christ. She knew that when I was being negative, I wasn't the person Lori had met about six months before—a person who was going to church every Sunday.

"I had accepted Christ, but I was doing nothing about my relationship with Him on a daily basis. Lori had noticed a difference not only in my attitude but also in my golf game. She encouraged me and challenged me. She said, 'I'll never tell you what to do, but I will tell you that you have changed, and I will tell you as your friend.' Then she said, 'I don't like it.'

"I thought to myself, *This is my mom talking to me.*"

By the time Wendy had reached the end of the fall semester of her sophomore year, Lori was ready to make a suggestion to her young protégé. She said, "Wendy, I'm going to ask you to do one thing for me. Go to one Fellowship of Christian Athletes meeting. If you don't like it, don't go back. Just do that one thing for me."

This appeared to be another one of those decision-making times for Wendy. Another crossroads when her decision affected her life for years to come. Out of respect for Lori, Wendy went.

"I walked in that room at the FCA meeting," Wendy recalls in amazement, "and if I didn't feel the Holy Spirit coming off every person! It was a powerful experience. I sat there that night and I said, 'You know what, Lord, I think You're calling for me.'"

She answered that call and committed her life completely to the Lord. "I haven't turned back since," she says.

Through it all—from that FCA recommitment through her latest Tour victory, Lori Brock has been one of Wendy's spiritual mentors. "She's one I've turned to. She's had some rough times in her life, and she's been able to get through those only because she has Somebody much more powerful to pull her through."

Brock, who is now the women's golf coach at the University of Tennessee, and Ward keep in touch throughout the golf season.

Wendy feels that the significance of her decision as a sophomore went beyond the spiritual. She feels that her crossroads decision at that point in her life also affected her golf game.

"About three months after that," she says, "I won my first college championship."

She says, "I basically did nothing to change my game. I wasn't practicing any more or less, and several people wanted to know what the difference was in the second half of my sophomore year.

"What a great way to witness to say, 'I've changed one thing in my life. I've changed the number one thing in life and otherwise, I can't explain anything more.' For people who were not Christians, that made no sense. I still use that when I talk to kids or when I talk to FCA groups. I try to tell them, 'God's got so much power that we cannot explain it in human terms.'"

Wendy Ward finds nothing odd about noticing the tie between her golf game and her walk with God. Another time in her life when she felt that the two were connected was during the US Amateur tournament in 1994. "This was a very special week," she says. "Not just in golf, but spiritually.

"I had been moved to be in the Bible that week. The tournament was in a smaller city—Roanoke, Virginia—and there were no distractions. I was reading about the fruit of the Spirit, and God was telling me about the fruit. This was a long week of golf. I played eleven rounds of golf in seven days. It was an entire week of needing extra patience. I had to learn how to pace myself and practice perseverance. Imagine how many things can go up and down in a round of golf, and then throw eleven rounds into one week's worth of play.

"Those words from Galatians spoke to me about not being quick to get angry or upset, but to be kind and gentle."

The tournament was very close, but Ward never doubted that she could win. Ahead with one hole to go and the US Amateur pretty much in hand, she stepped away for a moment to gather her thoughts.

"I walked off that thirty-fifth hole and kind of took a little time to myself. I wanted to quiet all my excited energy and give God some time. I wanted to give Him the credit. But I got interrupted in my prayer time. The president of the women's committee, Wilma Gilliland, came over to me and she said, 'Wendy, congratulations, but I have to ask you something. Will you be a part of our world women's amateur team?'

"This is a team with only three women on it. I was excited. I was in the middle of talking to God and trying to calm down—and now all of a sudden I've got this laid on my plate.

"I said, 'Well, I'm going to have to think about it.'

"She said, 'What do you mean, think about it?'

"You know, this was one of those things you don't have to think about. This is the highest honor you can receive as an amateur. I said, 'I've got to check my school schedule, because it's during school.'" Ward had one more year of college before her.

"The official said, 'No, no, no, I don't think you realize how important this is.'

"And I really didn't. But I said, 'I'll go. School will have to wait three days.'"

With that settled, Ward calmly went to the final hole and captured the US Women's Amateur tournament. "There was no doubt in my mind that I could win. Spiritually it was a very uplifting week and a very deep week."

A lot happened between the huge amateur victory in 1994 and that first professional win in 1997.

Yet what Wendy did after the big victory at the Fieldcrest Cannon win reveals one of the best things that happened to her along the way. After capturing that first win, Ward became a caddie.

But she was not a caddie for just anyone. She was carrying the bag of a very special golfer. A man named Nate Hair. A man she was engaged to be married to.

Hair, who also is a professional golfer, was scheduled to play in the Eastern Washington State Open, so Wendy went along to caddie.

Nate and Wendy had become friends in early 1996—somewhat as a surprise to her. "He was out there on the golf tour. I didn't know that's where God had him for me. About the time I was starting to think that God was going to make me the happiest single person around, he dropped Nate right in front of me."

He became a valuable resource for her as she tried to establish herself on the LPGA Tour. "It's been good to have another Christian—a Christian man to talk to about some of the frustrations.

"He's a pro golfer too, but it's a lot tougher for the guys. It's demanding and financially very difficult." Perhaps that's why he supplements his income as a caddie on the LPGA Tour.

"It's good for him to talk and get the frustrations out. For him to have a personal relationship with Christ is so important. It's good to hear him say to me, 'I care about you and your game, but you know who cares about it so much more than I ever could, and that's our Father in heaven.' To have that relationship is special. He can reach out to me, but when he does, I know it's God working through him."

Wendy Ward has stood at many crossroads in her life as a golfer. The decision whether to take her coach's advice and go to that vital FCA meeting. The choice to become engaged to Nate. The decision to forget about others and play golf to please the Lord. She has discovered that whenever it's decision-making time, God will, as her favorite Bible verse says, "make her paths straight."

That's a good thing for anyone standing at a crossroads to know.

Q & A WITH WENDY WARD

Q: *What is your favorite golf course?*
Wendy Ward: I represented the US on the Curtis Cup team, which is like our Ryder Cup team, only for amateurs. We played a course in Chattanooga. It is a paradise. You walk through a wooden gate into this paradise of a golf course. The owners, Jack and Alice Lupton, reserve this course for amateur tournaments.

Q: *What do you do on tour to stay sharp spiritually?*
Wendy: We have a fellowship on tour, and it is directed by Cris Stevens. She's been a counselor to both Nate and me as far as our relationship with each other and our relationship with Jesus Christ. We usually have our golfers' fellowship on Monday or Tuesday night. That's where we get fed—where God brings everything back into perspective.

Q: *What do you say to encourage young girls interested in golf?*
Wendy: The opportunities are rising for young girls. I think it's great that girls are feeling more comfortable in sports. I encourage girls to realize that there is an opportunity for them to get college golf scholarships. I've heard that three hundred women's golf scholarships go unused every year.

Q: *What goals do you have for yourself in golf?*
Wendy: I would love to enjoy the platform of being one of the top players on the LPGA Tour, if and only if that's what God has planned for me. I know He won't make me one of those top players if He doesn't feel like I can handle it. There are added pressures of being there. But it could also be a platform that He wants me to have to tell a little more about Him.

Q: *What do you do to get away from it all?*
Wendy: Nate has gotten me into fishing. It's a very relaxing hobby. The neat thing is that on some of the courses we play, you can take your gear out to the pond. There's a place in Youngstown, Ohio. It's called Avalon Lake. Fellow golfer Tracy Hanson got me to fish there. And that's where I caught my first fish. Also, Barb Mucha and I like to go bowling.

THE WARD FILE

LPGA Record

Year	Number of tourneys	Best finish	Money	Rank	Average strokes
1996	23	T9	$79,461	75	72.82
1997	24	1	$175,264	50	72.41

Moody Press, a ministry of Moody Bible Institute,
is designed for education, evangelization, and edification.
If we may assist you in knowing more about Christ
and the Christian life, please write us without obligation:
Moody Press, c/o MLM, Chicago, Illinois 60610.

DATE DUE

AP 2 '09			
AP 30 '09			

Demco, Inc. 38-293